MONIKA AND MARCIN GAJDA

PERSONAL DEVELOPMENT

HOW TO COOPERATE WITH GRACE?

CONTEMPLATIVE THERAPISTS
LOOK AT HOW TO GROW AS CHRISTIAN PERSONS

Contents

INTRODUCTION 1

PART I : "WHO AM I?" 7

  I. THE GOAL OF PERSONAL DEVELOPMENT 8

  II. WHAT IS LOVE? 20

  III. THE FALSE SELF 35

  IV. SELF-ESTEEM 43

PART II : "SELF-DEVELOPMENT" 58

  I. KNOWING ONESELF 59

  II. FEELINGS 64

  III.RELATIONSHIP WITH PARENTS 78

  IV. NEUROTIC PAIN AND GROWING PAIN 94

  V. WORKING WITH THOUGHTS 100

  VI. SMASHING THE "FALSE SELF" 113

  VII. CHANGES 123

  VIII. TYPOLOGY OF PERSONALITIES 132

  IX. SELF-LOVE 143

X. (CONCERN FOR THE GROWTH OF OTHERS) 151

XI. LOVE OF GOD (PRAYER) 155

XII. RESOLUTIONS...164

"They that sow in tears shall reap in joy" 168

Bibliography 170

TThe authors' websites in Polish: 175

NASZYM UKOCHANYM DZIECIOM:

PAWŁOWI, MIRIAM, JAKUBOWI I TYMOTEUSZOWI,

ABYŚCIE SZLI I OWOC PRZYNOSILI…

INTRODUCTION

Think about the extraordinary nature of the human being! We live where the spiritual and material worlds collide. Our bodies are composed of amino acids, just like the bodies of lizards, butterflies, and whales. We sweat, we nourish ourselves, we eliminate waste, our hair falls out, we gain weight, we lose weight, and we break bones. Sometimes our bodies are in pain, and at other times we feel good. There comes a point when these bodies die, and the billions of atoms that composed them decompose. If satisfying our hunger and thirst and gratifying our instinct to procreate were the extent of our potential and experience, biology would suffice to explain the meaning of our existence. This, however is not the case.

There are these strange places known as art galleries that we fill with things that are of no use to an ordinary animal. We generate, arrange, and combine sounds, and call this music. This likewise serves no practical purpose. We put up other strange buildings, not for anyone to live in, but for people to engage in what they call prayer. Most peculiarly however, some of us lovingly surrender our lives for our enemies, contrary to our survival instinct. This absurdity cannot be explained by Darwinian theory.

Indeed, we belong to a miraculous supernatural order, to the world of the spirit. This is most clearly expressed through our capacity for love and our responsiveness to beauty. Only humans can be moved to tears by reading poetry. Only humans climb mountains for no particular reason. Only humans can selflessly give to others. You might never have noticed the gospel verse that likens the kingdom of heaven to the yeast a woman mixed in with three measures of flour,[1] but this biblical parable is applicable to the nature of the human person. Everyone has three spheres: spirit, psyche (or soul) and body. Each is important and impacts the other two. They are the three measures of flour into which yeast has to be mixed for everything to rise. Only then can the bread that nourishes us be baked. This biblical yeast is the grace of God with which we can purposefully partner through self-development.

Grace! That's the word. It should not be omitted. We need to turn to grace if we want to write about personal development in its Christian conceptualization. Grace is a mysterious force. It is infinitely gentle, but at the same time, it is assertive and decisive. It is invisible but omnipresent, and it continually desires to propel us towards love. It overflows superabundantly, patiently awaiting our response. Grace is completely devoid of compulsion and authoritarianism. It does not coerce, but it summons us: "You can do it, you can do it... more, higher, wider, deeper[2]... You can contribute to the life of That From Whence everything originates..."

Grace is a miraculous gift to humankind from God.[3] It stands at the wellspring of our personal growth. If we want to blossom, it is because grace has been operating inside us. Our growth is consummated through grace and in conjunction with grace. We cannot effect anything on our own. The yeast is external. We would not ask for grace unless it had previously enabled us to do so.

---

[1] Cf. Matt. 13:33. All Biblical citations are from the New American Bible.

[2] Cf. Eph. 3:18.

[3] "Grace is a permanent state of miraculous communication with God. Grace is a miraculous gift from God to humankind as rational and free creatures. As a result, humankind is now a participant in the life of the triune God in the temporal world, albeit in a concealed and imperceptible manner (John 6:57; Eph. 2:18). It is also assured of attaining salvation, i.e. a final and eternal union with God (1 Cor. 13:12; 1 Pet. 1:3; 1 John 3:2)." Leksykon duchowości katolickiej [Lexicon of Catholic Spirituality], Fr. Marek Chmielewski (Ed.), M (Pub.), Lublin-Kraków 2002, p. 471. Authors' bolding.

The spirit, the body, and the psyche impact each other, and in a sense, permeate each other, although they do not intermingle. This order cannot be mixed up: The spiritual is spiritual, the physical is physical, and the emotional is emotional. The spiritual, however, is expressed through the body and the emotions. The corporeal affects sensibility and spirituality. Our personality affects how we function in the material world and which internal growth path we follow. However, the spirit, the psyche, and the body are not equivalent. The spirit is recognized as primal, as it is what makes each of us an exceptional person in this world.[4]

As spiritual beings, created from love and for love, humans are highly vulnerable. A person can be hurt by a word or by the lack of a word. And that's not all. A person can be hurt by being looked at and even by not being looked at. This is truly exceptional. No other creature on earth is this fragile. Had we not been created for love, evolution would have long since disposed of our (hyper)sensitivity as an unnecessary weakness.

As our lives do not end with the death of our bodies, and as they transcend the outwardly visible, the inner life is the life most relevant to human development. Our considered opinion, as therapists, is that only therapy that takes spirituality into consideration is appropriate for humans and therefore completely effective.[5] Every other approach diminishes the individual to a greater or lesser extent.

---

[4] Matt. 10:28. "And do not be afraid of those who kill the body but cannot kill the soul; rather, be afraid of the one who can destroy both soul and body in Gehenna".

[5] We consider the term "Christian therapy" fully justified. Any therapist who claims that her view of the world should not make any difference to the client has to know that this is in itself an expression of a particular worldview. As Christian therapists, we have our own approach to therapy, both from a philosophical perspective and in terms of healing techniques. This approach takes account of spirituality and the operation of grace. The views presented in this book constitute the basis of our comprehension of therapy, which can be defined as Christian Integrated Therapy.

Contemporary science has subscribed to the declaration that grace, insofar as it exists at all, has no influence on research or scientific results. Just like that. Only that which can be measured is said to be scientific. However, even such narrow fields as mathematics and physics are approaching limits in their development where the distinction between the measurable and the philosophical is becoming blurred. If that is the case, then how much more should psychology factor in spirituality?[6] Has anyone proven that the spirit and grace do not exist? The assumption that a person can achieve full integration and development without taking spirituality into consideration smacks of intellectual arrogance in view of the experience of all the great traditions and cultures. As Christians, we do not have to justify taking spiritual life and the operation of grace into account when considering human development. Rather, it behooves those who reduce the individual to the level of biology to show the basis on which they do so. Who lives in a deeper emotional peace? Westerners, consuming their tons of stimulants, tranquilizers, and psychotropic drugs? Or those people we sometimes hastily label as primitive? We constantly come across human stories that prove that the internal life affects emotional integration. The neuroses, depressions, addictions, compulsions, and mental illnesses from which our patients have suffered are all too frequently a consequence of their rejecting the spiritual dimension of life.

Religious people can likewise reveal immature attitudes. Statements such as: "Depressed? You just need to have more faith in Jesus and it'll all work itself out," are thankfully being heard less often, but religious believers have long tended to view psychology with mistrust. They either see it as a threat to their religion or with the fear that therapeutic practices may cause an evil spirit to enter

---

6 ..."Psyche" is the Greek word for "soul".

the person. In some circles, fear of the devil is so great that any therapeutic work is suspect. Even terms like "relaxation technique" can cause anxiety. Some teachers are constantly focused on spiritual dangers instead of proclaiming the victory of Jesus. Paradoxically, they thereby arrive at Manichaeism or a typically pagan magical thinking in Christian packaging, in which omnipotent evil is presumed to be lurking everywhere and an individual's conscious choices (a life in sacramental grace, a decision to follow Jesus, etc.) appear to be of secondary importance. That various phenomena sometimes thought to be spiritual (or supernatural) can be explained psychologically is also disconcerting to some. This is detrimental to spirituality, as spiritual reality can be rejected by those who, being cognizant of emotional phenomena, regard everything religious as "completely unenlightened."

There is a lack of understanding underlying these deeply suspicious attitudes. The originators of certain branches of psychotherapy were indifferent to religion. Some were even opposed to the Church. This, however, does not alter the fact that some of their achievements advanced psychology. A person who errs philosophically, and ever morally, can always stumble onto a grain of truth. Nowadays, it would be absurd to disregard accepted Freudian theories simply because he was not a practising Christian. Fencing ourselves in with mistrust would place us on the periphery of science. This is not to say, however, that we should uncritically accept everything we encounter in the various streams of psychotherapy.

There is in fact no conflict between theology and psychology. Finding a contradiction between these two fields would signal that an error had been made in theology and/or psychology. The longer we work on the boundary between these two fields, the greater is our fascination with the fact that there is only one truth. It can be described using a variety of scholarly languages, but this does not alter the fact that we are dealing with integral knowledge about people.

Humans are the only beings who simultaneously belong to the spiritual and the material world. Their inimitable beauty and their capabilities follow from this, but so do tension and the difficulty of existence. The greater the gift, the greater the effort that has to be put into using it appropriately. The development discussed in this book is a single process that embraces the entire individual: body, soul, and spirit.

We were created and we are continually becoming. And we have an impact on whom we become. If you wish to use this book for your personal becoming, then it will accomplish that objective. We welcome you to come on a journey with us into the depths of the human person.

Monika and Marcin Gajdowie

PART I

"WHO AM I?"

I.

THE GOAL OF PERSONAL DEVELOPMENT

Just as we cannot build a house without foundations, we cannot start work on our own development with a clear purpose unless we know where this development is meant to lead. When Jesus was asked which law was the most important in life, he unhesitatingly answered it was the commandment to love.[7] He chose this from among the 640 commandments in the Torah as that which sets human life on the right course. In the Christian conceptualization, an individual exists in order to love, and is only fulfilled when he loves.

> THE PURPOSE OF HUMAN
> DEVELOPMENT
> IS LOVE.

One could ask precisely why we set down love as the objective of human development. The answer is mystical: because God is love and the individual is meant to be united with God. God is the purpose of human life. Spirituality brings this extraordinary perspective before us. **Complete human development finds its expression in the individual loving like God loves, and participating**

---

[7] Cf. Matt 22:36-37.

in His internal life.[8] Therefore, anything that serves this ultimate end of union with God in love prods us in the right direction. St. John of the Cross said that we would be judged at the end of our lives on our love. The last judgment need not be understood as something happening externally from us. By rejecting the development towards love, we expose ourselves to suffering. Completely rejecting love puts a person in hell. The commandment to love is also the healthiest for the individual from a psychological standpoint. Anyone who aims for mature love automatically becomes more integrated and increasingly emotionally healthy.

> Disregarding love as the purpose of human development in therapy can retard and even be downright harmful to the therapeutic process, as the patient is very often in need of therapy precisely because he has been deprived of love. All emotional, and many psychological, disturbances (with the exception of those caused by biochemical imbalances) can be considered love disorders. The neurotic "loves" himself and others in a disordered way that damages himself and those around him. For us, therapy is therefore about getting the individual to start developing towards mature love. When that happens, the symptoms of the illness will pass, as they have only appeared because the individual has deviated from the right direction in life. It is our view that the symptoms serve to guide the individual to the right development path (that is, to mature love). They therefore have a most positive function. Our emotional self does not leave evidence to torture or humiliate us, but to lead us in the right direction.

The ultimate purpose of personal development is love. Therefore, any partial development, whether it be physical, emotional, material, intellectual, artistic, or religious, only makes sense insofar as it brings us closer to the main goal. If working on ourselves and perfecting some area or other does not serve love,

---

[8] In theology, this state is known as "deifying unification".

then from our Christian perspective, it ceases to be significant and can even become harmful.

Imagine someone who has attained the height of physical development and becomes an Olympic gold medalist, wins every triathalon, and achieves an extraordinarily shapely and athletic figure. All these achievements, while good in themselves, will only have an impact on the real development of the person who has made that effort in the service of love, and not from egocentrism. If physical development negates love (for example, by harming competitors, or through envy of them, or by wallowing in narcissism) then an Olympic gold medal around the neck of an athlete might well become a millstone drowning him in the sea.

Once the lights and cameras are turned off and the stands are empty, the individual finds himself alone with his darkness. This is not about any sanctimonious fear of "divine retribution," but a real, subjective, palpable feeling of defeat, distress, and detachment from life that will accompany him if he has invested all his efforts into developing his body, but has done so without subordinating these efforts to love.

At times we see people who have acquired superb communication skills. They brilliantly manage to set boundaries, convey their knowledge, and have excellent interpersonal skills. But, they will experience discomfort to a greater or lesser degree when love is not in the framework of their aim.

> THERE CAN BE NO MATURE LOVE
> WITHOUT AN ASSERTIVE ATTITUDE,
> BUT ASSERTIVENESS IN AND OF ITSELF
> IS NOT THE PURPOSE OF OUR
> DEVELOPMENT.

It is necessary to learn how to say "no" and to set boundaries and conditions in order to love properly. However, human development is not complete with the acquisition of assertiveness. The purpose of human development is love.

We occasionally meet people after therapy[9] who have consequently begun to set boundaries, realize their own goals in life, and take up completely new challenges, while experiencing a progressive deterioration of family relations as a result. Such was the case with a certain woman who was undergoing therapy in a ACA group,[10] and had asked us for help.

As a result of therapy, she had finally begun to look after herself, and no longer had the anxiety neurosis she had suffered for years. The positive changes were apparent, but her family system entered a temporary crisis, as family members got to know their "new" mother, wife, daughter-in-law, etc.

The crisis deepened quickly and there was no end in sight. The woman was very anxious about this because, as she put it, "Life was supposed to get better, but it's getting worse and worse." After our interview, we ascertained that this was not because those close to her did not want to respect the positive changes that had taken place, but because she had stopped her growth at assertiveness, not understanding that this attitude is hardly a point of departure for achieving the proper purpose of development, which is love. The woman had set boundaries as counselled in the ACA group, and although she had done it in accordance with the rules (with respect for others, firmness, etc.), the family was splitting further apart. This was especially true of her relations with her husband and her mother.

---

[9] For reasons of professional confidentiality, all the case histories described herein have had any identifying details altered to protect the privacy of the individuals concerned. Any resemblance to actual persons, living or dead, or actual events is purely coincidental.

[10] ACA: Adult Children of Alcoholics.

What did it matter that she had set boundaries and requirements if she did not consider that the people around her needed time to mature, that perhaps they could not instantly come to grips with certain issues, and that her octogenarian mother might not be able to change anything about herself at all? The woman who had come to us for help very quickly came to realize that, if she persisted in this course of action, she would have to leave her husband (whom she loved and who was not "pathological") and sever all contact with her mother, who was unable to respect her boundaries, and continued to treat her in a domineering manner as if she was a small child.

She therefore saw herself faced with the apparent dilemma of having to choose between being true to herself, and applying everything she had learned during therapy, which would mean the loss of those closest to her, giving up, and having to feel that she was betraying herself. This was driving her to despair. She was greatly relieved when we showed her a third option that she had not considered. This option was charitable love.

The woman understood that even if she gave up something (which she was already able to justify as a result of her personal therapy), she would still remain true to herself if she was doing it out of love. If she gave up something to give someone else a growth opportunity, then renouncing her legitimate rights would not be a defeat, but a victory. So long as it does not have to do with a fundamental issue, such as restricting freedom, inflicting violence, or threatening life or health, then anything can be given up without losing yourself.

She found peace of heart in this way. She smiled at herself and yielded in certain things, understanding that she was doing so out of love and with intrinsic freedom, and that this resignation on her part was not a sign of weakness, but on the contrary, of strength. **Love, not assertiveness, was the pinnacle** *she wanted to strive for. Relations with her husband and mother began to improve. Her husband began to change, but her mother, despite going to the* *grave unchanged, was correctly convinced that her daughter loved her.*

We often hear about someone who has achieved spectacular academic results and made great discoveries, but who is still a child in terms of interpersonal relations, who does not know how to bond with people, and who is either overbearing or withdrawn. Learning can become a form of escape or an attempt to exist in the world, but only love lets us bear the burden of existence and gives us a profound feeling of happiness and sense of being.

It is clear that wealth and fame often do not serve an individual's ultimate purpose. These things are not bad in themselves, but they can close us off to love. And while it may come as a surprise to some, **an increase in religiosity might not serve love either**. In fact, it might even push love away. Let's take a quick look at this.

Humans are religious by nature. This does not generally need to be justified; it is enough to peruse the history of humanity. Atheism merely confirms the existence of a common religious instinct. This is because being an atheist entails the rejection of something that is to some extent in our very make up. Most people sense the existence of a Higher Power. Religious ritual is a positive thing, and it emanates from the deep human conviction that a Reality exists that is greater and more profound than anything around us, and that being human is something more than being a biologically processing entity. The individual cannot understand herself without this Power, which has been named and represented in a variety of ways in different cultures through the ages.[11] The religiousness of all peoples is an expression of humanity's place in the order of

---

[11] It should be noted that the less literal the attempt to define divinity, the clearer it is. The gradual revelation of God through the ages eventually led to a discernment of SOMEONE whose name could not be uttered and the rendering of whose image was forbidden. Then Jesus transferred the worship of God from stone temples to human hearts. In this manner, the Revelation achieved its apex and completeness in the Man who Loves us to the end. The Man became the image of the unseen God.

creation: there is SOMETHING else; there is SOMEONE else. **The Mysterious Power, ever present in the collective consciousness and established by the human family throughout history, is constantly inviting us to enter into the inner life**. Religiousness is valuable, as it creates space for the self-revelation of the force that interferes ever deeper in human life and which designates itself the ultimate purpose of human existence. Religion also feeds on the wonder of creation. This wonder is a natural contemplative experience. All these can be called the **positive sources of religiousness**.[12]

A person surrounded by the beauty of creation can nevertheless experience tremendous isolation. This stems from having been "separated from the Father," which is known as original sin in the Christian tradition. The fundamental emotion associated with humanity after this tragic "fracture" is angst. Adam answered God's call: "Where are you?" with "…I was afraid because I was naked…"[13] Angst can inspire religiousness, which helps keep it under control. The wellsprings of inner life are then poisoned and the ritual built on this religiousness does not lead to freedom and development, but to a stunting of the person. These are the **negative sources of religiousness**. Karl Marx correctly observed that religion was the opiate of the masses, as in a sense it let the world be domesticated and the angst of existence, which is really a fear of passing away and final annihilation, be mitigated.

---

[12] We can therefore speak of a natural (i.e. innate) aesthetic contemplation that, apart from intellectual (philosophical), emotional, corporal and theological contemplation, constitutes a major step towards supernatural (infused) contemplation.

[13] Cf. Gen. 3:9-10.

And now we come to something very important:

> RELIGIOUSNESS CAN LEAD A PERSON TO LOVE, BUT IT CAN ALSO BE A STUMBLING BLOCK TO DEVELOPMENT, IF IT BECOMES NOTHING MORE THAN A SUPERSTITIOUS RITUAL OR IS USED FOR PURPOSES THAT ARE NOT SPIRITUAL

If a person stops at exterior religiosity, it might be easy to fall into the trap of empty ceremonies that feed on habit, tradition, patriotism, fear, and so on. A person who diminishes religion this way can even kill for religious reasons and find himself in opposition to God.

A young Catholic man came to us for help with intensified OCD, which had gradually prevented him from working and fulfilling his family responsibilities. He was an accountant, and for him, this meant interminable fear of having made a mistake in the accounts. It gradually became impossible to work, as what would normally have taken him an hour was now taking several hours and causing a great deal of emotional strain. Moreover, his uneasiness about having made a mistake was harming other people, the company, and the country.

When we interviewed him, we found that religious tension had dogged him for years, but he had never treated it as anything to worry about, as he considered it an expression of his faith in God. He confessed the same sins repeatedly, as he could never be sure that he had confessed correctly. The minute he left the confessional, he would have qualms about having held back some sin. He therefore practically never received communion. After all, he might have been committing a mortal sin. He fasted on Fridays, as his fear of eating meat had assumed such proportions that he was too scared to eat at all, as anything he might have eaten could have touched "forbidden" food. He didn't use cutlery on days of fasting out of fear that the utensils might have had meat on them. He was so scared of slacking in his morning and evening devotions that he dragged out his prayer ritual endlessly.

It turned out that the religiosity of our patient's mother, who also lived in constant fear of God, played a special role in the origin of his neurotic symptoms. She frightened him with hell when he was a small child. The woman wanted to raise him as a "good moral Christian," and so instilled a fear of sin and God into him. Our patient pictured the Creator constantly monitoring people and writing down every stumble and fall in a great book.

The mother did not allow her son to express anger and stifled him with, "Honor your father and your mother," thereby depriving him of any chance of protestation. Our client was also afraid of sexual feelings, because Jesus said, "everyone who looks at a woman with lust has already committed adultery with her in his heart."[14]

Curiously, our patient's mother was heavily involved in political activity and was known for her aggressive language. She saw no contradiction between the gospel and the way she behaved in her own life. It was obviously to us that there was an unenlightened fear, and not a love of truth, behind her "radicalism."

Bottled-up feelings, combined with excessive thought about hell and a false image of God, were at the root of the neurosis that was tormenting our client. He was going to need more time to build trust in a new and unfamiliar religious focus of purpose. Significantly, he knew us from our work in the church, so he knew that he wasn't coming to people who were going to give him answers along the lines of "Give up Catholicism and your problems will go away," although his deliverance did in fact require a temporary cession of various religious practices. With the assistance of the priest, who understood the nature of the problem, we were able to help him considerably. Our client also had to

---

[14] Mt. 5:28.

become friends with his own sensibility, and accept the anger he displayed (especially towards his mother), and his sexual feelings. But unless a valid focus of religious purpose was restored and love identified as the beginning and end of a religious life, all this was going to prove very difficult, if not impossible.

Religion is not just supposed to deaden the pain of existence and assuage the fear of death, although it can be reduced to this, as happened in this particular case. **However, it would be most unjust to say that religion is nothing more than a response to fear.**

> JESUS LEADS HUMANITY AWAY FROM RELIGION (OUTWARD DEVOTION BASED ON LAW) AND TOWARDS SPIRITUALITY (INNER DEVOTION BASED ON GRACE).

The teacher from Nazareth said that the time was at hand when God would no longer be worshipped on any mountain or in any temple. True worshippers would worship in spirit and in truth.[15] Obviously, this did not mean that religious ritual and organized worship were no longer relevant. Jesus himself continued to go to the synagogue. **Genuine and profound spirituality always shows respect for religious displays, both for the tradition that has given rise to them and for other religious traditions.** However, Jesus taught that religion only fulfilled its function insofar as it guided people towards an inner experience that ultimately segued into contemplation that leads to union with God. External worship is like a body for the soul. So long as we live in the material world, we need outwardly expressed rituals. **Spirituality transcends religion in the same way that the soul transcends the body.** God transcends all religious traditions and cannot be limited to a single religious

---

[15] Cf. John 4:23.

confession. God is neither Jew nor Muslim. Nor is he Christian, as hard to believe as some might find this.

Increasing numbers of Christians leaving the practice of their faith is too easily explained by "bad times" and/or the atheization and secularization of culture, supported by forces hostile to religion. Obviously the enemy never sleeps, but has not every generation of those seeking to follow Christ faced similar challenges?

Might it not be the case that people leave their religion because they cannot find any spirituality in it? They probably instinctively feel that spiritual reality cannot be experienced as trivially and superficially as it so often is in their everyday church life. Why would they persist with religion when it is insufficient in itself, doesn't explain anything, and doesn't go anywhere? If Christians see themselves and their purely secular neighbours as equally good people, or perhaps they find a more loving, humanitarian response outside the church than within it, they might quickly conclude there is no point in going to church services, unless they were to find deep spirituality. We find this mentality latent in the average congregation. It has even come to the paradoxical situation in which worship, which is supposed to lead to mysticism and union with God, is sometimes offered in such a perfunctory and peremptory manner that it would take a mystic to discern anything divine in it. It is no wonder then that the bored and despondent begin to look elsewhere for transcendence, or simply abandon the search and chase after pleasures that bring a little relief. People cannot desire a reality they cannot see and do not know. And they cannot see and do not know a transcendent reality because nobody shows it to them. If people were to experience the miraculous, nobody could make them turn away from religion. That is because the corpse is found where the vultures descend.[16]

Religion, when lived shallowly, fuelled by fear of sickness, unhappiness and death, begins to obscure The One who desires to lead the individual towards love. **Immature religion can became an obstacle to personal growth**, both for its practitioners and those "on the outside."[17]

> OUTWARD WORSHIP SHOULD ALWAYS LEAD TO LOVE, OTHERWISE RELIGION BECOMES INEFFECTIVE AND EVEN DOWNRIGHT HARMFUL.

Religion, in the hands of worldly rulers, can be weaponized, turned into a policy tool, and made a means of hindering social development and manipulating people, promoting and disseminating hatred, instead of guiding the progress of the human family. **Limiting religion this way, to become merely the means to desired goals – even if the goals are noble social or political ones – is in fact the degradation of religion, because religion's true goals are transcendent**. Religion can also be injurious to the emotional health of its practitioners when it is distorted and based on false theological premises.

[16.]Cf. Luke 17:37.

[17.]This is why Jesus addressed Peter harshly as follows: "Get behind me, Satan. You are thinking not as God does, but as human beings do." (Mark 8:33)

II.

WHAT IS LOVE?

Because personal growth is meant to guide us towards love, we need to know with clarity what love is. How can we tell that we are dealing with love? How does love affect its object?

If God is love, then any attempt to define the word is beyond human capabilities. For our purposes, we extract a particular aspect of love and give our own definition as follows, mindful of its deficiencies:

> LOVE IS AN ACT DIRECTED TOWARDS
> THE GOOD OF ANOTHER PERSON

Let us now take a closer look at what this definition means.

1. LOVE IS AN ACT

Love is an act, i.e. a specific activity, that may or may not be performed. **Love is not the feelings** with which it is very often confused. Love can be sustained by a variety of feelings, and not just pleasant ones (such as friendship, infatuation, or warmheartedness), but also by some normally regarded as "negative" (such as anger or envy). Will (choice, decision) and intellect (right thinking) determine whether a feeling moves someone towards love. A lack of choice or right thinking often leads to disaster.

Love can, however, be expressed through feelings. Pure and properly lived emotionalism goes hand in hand with love. As we develop, we act ever more rarely against our feelings, and ever more frequently we love and feel love in a single action. We have to consider what serves love, what acts are capable of being ordered to love, and what an act of love is all about. Love can be likened to a bird in that it has two wings. Both are needed to fly to its destination: the first wing is an affirmation, the second a requirement.

> LOVE IS EXPRESSED THROUGH AN
> AFFIRMATION AND A REQUIREMENT.

An affirmation flows from the very depths of the soul. Only someone with a genuinely loving heart immersed in God can make authentic affirmations. Love allows another person to **subjectively** experience being loved. When an affirmation is genuine, it bears upon every aspect of human nature – physical, emotional, and spiritual. The heart cannot be deceived; a genuine affirmation is more than mechanically uttering words and/or making gestures at the behest of the mind. An affirmation cannot be rehearsed. It is a gift both for the person making it and the person for whose benefit it is made. It is expressed in a tender glance, a gesture, a word, and sometimes in silence. **A genuine affirmation is a mystical experience**: it astounds the person who loves and the person who is loved. In actuality, it is God who affirms. We merely create space for His love. An affirmation is something beautiful and pleasant, deeply moving and touching.

*People pay us for our time in our office, but they cannot buy our hearts. Our hearts are priceless and we can only offer them ourselves. The heart cannot be bought or sold. **There can be no effective assistance for another person without an affirmation at the*** *very deepest level. We have often experienced mysterious moments when something opens up between us and a person in need. Something that could not have been anticipated and which has nothing to do with our knowledge or mastery of therapeutic techniques. This cannot be planned for. All that can be done is to pray for this experience and create the space for a meeting within ourselves.*

It appears when we are ready: the mystical moment, the extraordinarily intensive meeting with another person, leaning over the mystery of his suffering and development with full respect; complete acceptance and emotion that brings time to a standstill; the unquestionable and unnamed presence of the grace that heals wounds.

The moment of a deep affirmation is hard to describe. We know that this is IT when we receive one. It is often the therapeutic breakthrough when it happens in our office. It is sometimes associated with an immediate and complete cure. An affirmation is God among us.

The second wing of love, without which love cannot mature, is a requirement. **We lay down requirements precisely because we love, not despite the fact. Not laying down requirements is often a defect in love. People often confuse unconditional love with love without requirements.** "Since God loves me as I am, I don't have to change anything and others should accept me," they think. However, this is not true. Jesus did not come into the world to reduce the image of God to the size of a compact human heart, but to deify humanity. Love transports upwards and does so by, among other things, laying down requirements. When we love someone, we do not overlook an inconvenient truth to maintain a friendly atmosphere at the cost of the quality of a relationship. We do not shy away from saying difficult things or pointing out the necessity of making an effort. Laying down requirements can incur opposition, as they are unpleasant to both the giver and the receiver of the love.

Jesus shattered the peace and called a spade a spade repeatedly. This was not easy for his listeners and was sometimes met with fierce opposition. The Teacher spoke of the effort that had to be made to follow Him. God did not come into the world to be pleasant to us, but to raise us to the dignity of children of God: free and loving.

Setting boundaries and laying down requirements for those we love sometimes requires an enormous effort, as it carries the risk of rejection. Love can suggest letting someone into our home, even though he has let us down yet again. On another occasion, it can tell us to put his suitcase outside the door. Love does not offer a single, simple solution.

We have lost count of the number of times we have spoken to people who expressed surprise that love could demand words and/or gestures that inflicted pain on those they loved. We remember one conversation with a man, who had repeatedly been cheated on by his wife. She had had two children by him and another by her lover. The woman lived in two homes: sometimes with her husband; sometimes with the other man. This bizarre situation had already gone on for several years. Our patient was a wealthy man and his wife was evidently using him materially. She also hit him, which he allowed, because he understood love to mean forgiving, "not seven times: but seventy times seven," that is, indefinitely. Having been brought up by a very religious mother and grandmother, he could not imagine any option for a Christian husband other than to forgive and accept once more regardless of what had been done. It got to the stage where his sons stood up for him and hated their mother. She did not change her attitude in the slightest, and when he tried to talk to her, she would shut him up by mentioning the sanctity of marriage, knowing that he had no comeback to this. When she was in a better mood, she would actually apologize, although this did not prevent her from going back to her lover. When her mood worsened, she challenged him and resorted to throwing punches.

*Our client was very surprised when we told him that, in our view, he did not love his wife, because he had been sustaining her selfishness for years. He had never considered that, although God loves us just as we are, there are those who cannot obtain absolution for their sins until they change their behavior, or that nobody can receive holy communion unconditionally. What surprised him most was canon law,[18] where he read that separation was allowed in the case of adultery on the part of a spouse. He had never considered that **separation could be accepted as an expression of loving** and fighting for his wife. It was only after our discussion that he realized that a Christian marriage is not a form of slavery, and that its sacramental dimension does not necessitate being with the other person no matter how she behaves. He understood that he could remain faithful to his wife without condoning her actions.*

Another case that comes to mind is that of a single mother raising a 14-year-old son. Her son hit her because she had cut off his internet access after he had infringed every possible web usage rule. When we asked what happened next, we were really surprised to hear that her son went to bed, and that she made him breakfast and drove him to school the next day. When we asked her why she did this for a son who had hit her, she replied, "The child cannot go to school hungry, and it's so far away, and going by public transportation would take considerably longer...". You can judge our patient's understanding of maternal love for yourself.

Love is like a bird in that it cannot fly on one wing. **An affirmation is not enough on its own. Nor are requirements enough on their own. Both are necessary.** St. Paul wrote about this very thing in his "Hymn to Love".[19] The apostle mentions acts of extraordinary heroism – of giving away entire fortunes and even surrendering to death, stressing that all this could be done without love. Without affirmations (when I protect someone materially without giving my

---

[18.]The ecclesiastical law of the Catholic Church.

[19.]Cf 1 Cor. 13:1-13.

heart) and requirements (when the person for whom I am "burning myself out" remains selfish), there is no love. St Paul writes that love is kind, patient, and is not given to anger. True? Of course! We next read in the gospels that Jesus made a whip out of chords, glared at people, and called them "whitewashed sepulchres." This is also true of love.

2. LOVE IS AN ACT DIRECTED TOWARDS...

Love is realized in relationships. This is not a philosophical curiosity – it has practical implications for us. Because love is "always directed towards..." personal growth, we are going to examine it in the context of relations with other people. If we want to feel better, realize our goals and dreams, and deepen our inner life, that is, if we want to start working on ourselves, then we cannot lose sight of the objective which is the good of the other person.

> THE AIM OF DEVELOPMENT
> IS NOT PERFECTION
> BUT LOVE.

How does your neighbor benefit from you working on your own self-development, and starting to feel better, deepening your inner life, and eliminating faults and negative tendencies? Severing our inner efforts from the real and concrete good of others is a dangerous trap. Once we become our own goal (which is nothing but selfishness), we are like someone looking far ahead and seeing his own back. We lose the essential purpose of what we are doing, like a dog chasing its tail.

It should be borne in mind that love should be the motivation for embarking on self-development, and that we therefore need to develop ourselves for the good of others and not just to satisfy our own egos. When we work on self-development, we can fail to notice if we are revolving around ourselves.

Take for example someone suffering from compulsive sexual behavior. People thus afflicted often think of virtually nothing else and are solely preoccupied with the struggle to avoid failing the next time. The struggle for purity is obviously extraordinarily essential and noble, but it can subtly become selfish. We recognize this when someone is waging the battle by deploying only defensive strategies (avoiding doing anything negative) and falls into despair when she fails yet again. What might seem strangest of all is that, despite having failed hundreds of times, she is not a humble person and continues to judge others harshly. Overall, the worst sin she would own to is masturbation. That is the only sin she would confess – going from "blunder to blunder." However strange it might seem, we occasionally like to ask someone self-oppressed like this: "How would the world benefit if you stopped masturbating? Who would receive more love from you? And could you give this love today? Even despite your degeneracy? **Perhaps you'd be better off going to heaven repentant and small because of your sexual compulsion, which you genuinely don't want to give in to, rather than going to hell because of serving only your pride?** *And seeing as you can't stop right now, what can you take on that would be achievable? What good is waiting to be received? This obviously does not mean that you have to surrender to impurity." This line of conversation alters her perspective and paves the way to be freed from addiction more quickly.*

Our own development cannot be detached from the welfare of our neighbors. When we want to check whether we are loving properly, we should consider what those closest to us – family, friends, colleagues, and acquaintances – would say about us. Would they say that they have received kindness from us? Do we place our spiritual endeavours in their context? Or are our efforts and strivings focused exclusively on ourselves?

3. Love is an act directed towards **the good of another person.**

The opportunity to develop is one of the greatest gifts that true love has to offer. If you want to check whether you really love someone, spend some time thinking about the positives that have come into her life as a result of your love. **If you are dealing with genuine love, the recipient of that love will grow, or at least have an opportunity to grow, internally**. We obviously have no influence over whether someone we love will take up self-development, but love offers that opportunity. Whether or not it is utilized is entirely up to the other person.

> LOVE IS AN ACT THAT AIDS THE DEVELOPMENT OF ANOTHER PERSON.

One woman told us: "I loved my son so much that I devoted my life to him. When he was little, I followed at his heels, so that nothing would happen to him. When he was in school, I brought him snacks at every break. When he was in high school, I always waited for him, so that he didn't come home alone. And when he was in college, I moved to the other end of the country with him to clean and cook for him, so that he would have time to study. I simply cannot understand why he hates me, why he's gay and alcoholic... After I've loved him so much..."

This person felt something towards her son and called that something love. She did not, however, love him within the meaning of our definition, as their relationship was not conducive to his maturity. She herself had not developed. **Motherhood and fatherhood, when done properly, improve parents as well as children.**

Because love is conducive to development, a man who cheats on his wife does not really love his lover, although he may be convinced that he does. Nobody has ever developed through betrayal. Similarly, young people who sleep together with no strings attached do not really love each other; they are taking something from each other that they will never be able to give back in the event that they part ways. If they genuinely loved each other, they would take care to foster the virtue of chastity. This would pay dividends in their marital life, as the ability to exercise sexual restraint is an important component of an integrated and mature personality.

THE RELATIONSHIP OF LOVE DEVELOPS
BOTH THE PERSON LOVING AND THE
PERSON LOVED.

It sometimes happens that people live with an apparent dilemma: "Either I look after myself at the expense of someone else, or I look after someone else to my own disadvantage." If you have ever found yourself this situation, then you have made a mistake due to a misunderstanding of the good that love bestows. If you understand "good" to mean personal growth, then the situation would have appeared as follows: either you and the person with whom you had the problem could have followed the path of growth and progress, or the two of you could have abandoned any attempt to grow and become infantilized. We are never faced with the dilemma of "my growth and progress" at the expense of yours, or vice versa. This dilemma does not exist with true love. It is simply necessary to correctly interpret what this growth depends on. One final, but very important, word of caution: growth is not always pleasant. Love does not necessarily lift the mood of those we love.

We recall a 34-year-old woman, the youngest of five siblings, who came to us for help with worsening bouts of depression and suicidal thoughts that had been tormenting her for some time. She still lived with her parents, against whom she harboured a great deal of resentment, despite having had a good job for years. She wanted to move out, but was firmly convinced that, as the youngest of five siblings, she was obliged to take over their farm.

Her parents had "programmed" her future and even had their house specially designed for their youngest child to stay with them in their old age. Our patient was emotionally distraught, because she felt that leaving home would be a betrayal of her parents, for whose care she was responsible.

A man had come into our patient's life a couple of years previously. He had proposed to her, but she had not yet accepted. Her parents had not considered the possibility that their daughter would get married and leave home. The woman snuck out to date her would-be husband. After a while, she moved in with him, but she kept going back home with an enormous feeling of guilt and an empty heart. She did not have the strength to either accept or refuse a marriage proposal from the man she loved. She believed that her love for her parents required her to stay home with them, at least until they died, but her "boyfriend" would not even hear of living under the same roof as his in-laws.

Our patient needed to understand what true love was. Only then could she begin to make changes in her life. When we explained that **love leads to growth**, she began to consider what was happening in her life and the lives of those dearest to her. She understood that her love for her parents required her to move out, as only that would force them to face up to being "empty nesters." She also understood that she alone was responsible for her own personal growth and should not assume responsibility for how her parents would live. The curious thing was that her decision to leave home, once made, not only displeased her parents, but also her siblings, who suddenly realized that looking after the parents should be a burden shared equally among all the children.

The sense of guilt was constraining our patient. She learned to ignore it, knowing that it was based on a misunderstanding of love.

Obviously, it can happen that someone we love will construe our attitude as a lack of love, as he does not want to make the necessary effort to grow. **A person drifting on an ice floe will sometimes expect a rescuer to jump onto the ice with him. But no rational person should rescue someone close to them this way**. What the castaway hears is, "Grab the rope." Still, not everyone understands this and many cry out with resentment: "If he really loved me, he'd jump onto the ice floe to rescue me." That has to be met with: "It's precisely because I love you that I can't do it. You have to come out on to terra firma. I'm throwing you a line. You can catch it!" Experience shows that this response does not always meet with understanding. **Love creates a space for growth and propels us towards it, but it does not guarantee that the person loved will commit to that growth.** Whether he will eventually catch the line or stay there feeling resentful, and even unloved, is up to him.

When we think of love and growth, we are looking at a delightful mystery:

> GENUINE GROWTH LEADS TO EVEN GREATER LOVE, AND REAL LOVE LEADS TO GROWTH.

This marvellous positive reciprocal coupling continuously reinforces itself: growth => greater love => faster growth => greater love and so on ad infinitum, until being united with God. And because God, who is love, is infinite, our growth probably has no limits, even in eternity.

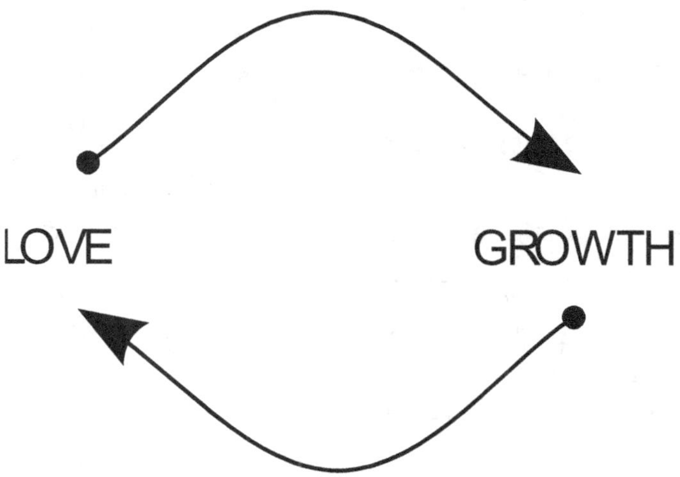

Anyone who sets out on the road to growth and does not deviate from it, will progress increasingly faster, just as a stone falling to earth moves increasingly faster under the force of gravity. This is the secret of the great saints whose lives experienced spiritual momentum. **If you cannot see this increase in love inside you, it might mean that your inner life is not properly "arranged."** It is worth giving this some thought.

You might be thinking: "You're always writing about growth and loving your neighbor, but what about happiness? I want to be happy and to have a good life. Write something about happiness!" We have some good news for you: **We have a right to happiness!**

"If I only lived somewhere else, had another job, looked different, was healthier, came from a different family, and had other people around me, then I would be happy. If only my life situation were different...." A lot of people think this way, thinking that "happiness is when you are happy." To them, happiness is like having a winning lottery ticket, and they have no influence on those winning numbers. But this is not the case.

How do we achieve a sense of happiness and fulfilment in life? Let's begin with three pitfalls that can waylay us in our quest for happiness. Fall into one of these, and you will never find happiness.

THREE PITFALLS ON THE ROAD TO HAPPINESS:
1. EQUATING HAPPINESS WITH PLEASURE
2. TRYING TO ACHIEVE HAPPINESS THROUGH EXTERNAL ACTIVITIES
3. OVERLOOKING THE INDIVIDUAL IN THE SEARCH FOR LOVE

1. EQUATING LOVE WITH PLEASURE

This mistake brings the negative consequences that come with avoiding all unpleasant difficulties. Because **there can be no growth without difficulties, avoiding unpleasantness carries the risk of infantilism**. Another adverse consequence of falling into this pitfall is that we commit all our activities to the goal of experiencing as much pleasure as possible, in order to be happy. Because pleasure is commonly identified with happiness, almost every advertisement alludes to it. A person who succumbs to this delusion will do anything to make product = pleasure = achieved happiness true, and wear herself out in the pursuit of inconsequential and non-essential things. Some people realize very late in life, sometimes just before death, that they have made a vital mistake. **There is nothing wrong with experiencing pleasure, but happiness does not depend on it. I can be happy without experiencing pleasure. We are called to happiness, but not to pleasure**. The pursuit of pleasure does not satisfy the heart.

2. TRYING TO ACHIEVE HAPPINESS THROUGH EXTERNAL ACTIVITIES

Anyone who falls into this trap will either arrange the world around himself so as to become happy, or deem this an impossibility in his current circumstances. This is why people keep looking for something outside themselves, such as an ideal place, an unforgettable moment, a special item, beautiful surroundings, "the one" person, or stimulants. They want to feel happy for a while. People have a yearning for profound peace and fulfilment, but they mistakenly look for it outside themselves. The state of "liberation" is so appealing that people are prepared to resort to drugs, alcohol, casual sexual relationships and passions to experience it for a moment. But this "liberation" only lasts for a moment and is only an imitation of what we experience permanently in a genuinely happy life. A sense of happiness has very little in common with an ecstatic and transitory emotional boost.

3. OVERLOOKING OTHER PEOPLE IN THE SEARCH FOR LOVE

Many would like to preserve their own "little world," cutting themselves off from other people and even annihilating them. Anyone "foreign" or "other" is potentially dangerous, as she might turn out to be a competitor for the too few available resources. Some seek their own happiness in the absence of others.[20] They "liberate themselves" in their desire to maintain their independence from others, and sink into loneliness. Happiness cannot be built on human injury and injustice.

How then can we attain happiness? **Happiness is a by-product of growth. To some extent, it appears together with the opportunity for love,** and it depends on our broadening our awareness,

---

[20] Jean-Paul Sartre: "L'enfer, c'est des autres" (Hell is other people).

deepening our harmony with all of creation, mindfulness[21] and peace of heart. **Happiness comes from being united with God.** By growing and developing (and so loving more and more), we achieve the sense of happiness, meaning and fulfilment that we yearn for. Happiness is therefore not something that is given to or withheld from anyone "in advance."

WE ACHIEVE HAPPINESS BY MAKING
A SELFLESS GIFT OF OURSELVES FOR
OUR NEIGHBOR.

Our personal growth leads in this direction. **The more we live for the** other, **the faster the** self **matures.** This paradox is due to **happiness being found when we do not seek it for ourselves.** Those who do everything possible to possess happiness will never find it. The road to happiness is unexpectedly revealed when we forget about ourselves.

[21.]The concept of "mindfulness" comes from depth psychology and denotes the focus of the senses and the intellect on what is. Mindfulness consists in consciously enduring the "here and now" of the present moment.

III.

THE FALSE SELF

Ever since original sin, we have all found ourselves in that peculiar state of confusion that comes from being cut off from Love. Not even the most wonderful parents can love us as much as God does. All parents make small and not-so-small mistakes with their children, and while they do so out of ignorance rather than malice, the results are still hurtful. From the moment we are born, we are never loved by anybody to our heart's satisfaction.

Imagine a little girl who has learned that her daddy has left home for another woman. What must she be feeling? How about a boy molested by his own mother? What must he be feeling? How does a child feel when she has to bring a drunk parent home in full view of all the neighbors? What does a child go through when she is beaten or only loved conditionally (in exchange for getting something from her), and who never hears words full of love? What must a child be going through when she is derided and ridiculed by her entire class at school or is rejected by her peers? How does a child feel when she gets the impression that she is not loved as much, or treated as well, as her brothers and sisters?

Even if we have not experienced anything as drastic as alcoholism, divorce, physical violence or sexual molestation in childhood, a minor parental quarrel may have seriously disturbed our feelings of security. It is enough to ask ourselves how we would feel if the unity of the Holy Trinity suddenly disintegrated. How unsettled would our world be if we were to learn that God was not love? That he was selfish and fragmented? Well, that is exactly how a child feels when the two people closest to her start to fight.

We have all found ourselves having to somehow manage in adverse situations. We were created out of love and for love, but we have all come up against a world that diverges from the ideal. **If she is going to survive, the child has to develop an individual defense mechanism that involves turning a blind eye to what is going on.** The child begins to behave in a characteristic way, to adopt specific strategies, and to start functioning on an emotional knee-jerk level that enables her to survive. In an extreme situation, the child could stop developing or even die unless she develops a defense mechanism. Initially, then, it is essential, and even lifesaving. In adulthood, however, it begins to be a hindrance and leads to negative consequences. What once enabled her to conceal herself now becomes a prison from which it is difficult to escape. **We call the defense mechanisms acquired in childhood, and the distinctive emotional, intellectual and social functioning that result from them "THE FALSE SELF".**[22]

---

[22] The FALSE SELF defense mechanisms are described more fully in the chapter "Typology of Personalities."

> "THE FALSE SELF" IS THE FALSE IDENTITY OF AN INDIVIDUAL THAT PREVENTS HER FROM ENTERING INTO A FRUITFUL RELATIONSHIP WITH HERSELF, HER FELLOW HUMAN BEINGS, AND GOD. IT IS GENERATED BY DEFENSE MECHANISMS ACQUIRED IN CHILDHOOD.
> "LIFE IN THE FALSE SELF" IS A SPECIFIC DEFENSIVE, EMOTIONAL, INTELLECTUAL AND SOCIAL FUNCTIONING, WHOSE RESULT IS A GREATER OR LESSER LOSS OF CONTACT WITH REALITY (A CONSTRICTION OF CONSCIOUSNESS).

> "THE REAL SELF"
> IS THE GENUINE IDENTITY OF AN INDIVIDUAL, AND IT ENABLES HER TO LOVE HERSELF, HER FELLOW HUMAN BEINGS, AND GOD.
> "LIFE IN THE REAL SELF"
> IS LIFE IN TRUTH,
> IN FULL FREEDOM, IN TOUCH WITH OUR OWN VALUES, AND IN THE REAL WORLD (A BROADENING OF CONSCIOUSNESS).

Every individual functions in the FALSE SELF to a greater or lesser extent when starting out in life. The roots of the FALSE SELF go very deep. They reach right back to the very beginnings of life, possibly even to the fetal stage, as the child is exposed to stress and rejection during this period. THE FALSE SELF therefore becomes our day-to-day means of functioning until the moment we consciously cease to develop it. Unless someone decides to work on self-development, the worst case scenario eventuates: the individual identifies with the FALSE SELF without realizing that she is dealing with a suite of defense mechanisms that first appeared in childhood. The FALSE SELF becomes a false identity. In this way, the individual can live completely cut off from herself in an unreal world where her thoughts, feelings, and choices spring from a mere defense strategy that has no existence in reality. Many people – indeed a clear majority of people in Western societies – live in a peculiar state of unconsciousness. By not having access to herself, and by living in the FALSE SELF, the individual does not have access to the other person or to God, as HE IS. This is the tragedy of the individual in the wake of original sin. In psychological terms, we could say that this is the root cause of neuroticism.

All the FALSE SELF mechanisms can be summarized in the following sentence: "I do not deserve to be loved as I am, and therefore need a disguise." The FALSE SELF makes the individual conceal herself from God and other people. The primary emotion that she feels is shame. This results in the most diverse strategies being adopted: one will avoid people, another will be "the life of the party." It does not matter that the former never sets foot outside the home, and might even tell herself that she is shy, while the latter is a wag who is seen everywhere. In both cases, the motivation for adopting the specific persona is a failure to accept themselves as they are, and this results in their trying to conceal themselves. They are both in thrall to the FALSE SELF, which becomes a powerful force that determines how they function.

When animals are afraid, they flee or attack. People behave exactly the same way when they feel anxiety. Some will withdraw into a world of their own and try to defend it at all costs. This will be a world that is limited (often to their own armchairs and TV sets), sometimes to their hobbies, interests and passions, such as garden plots, sports, and even religion, which can give the appearance of life, but which is in reality no more than a form of escapism. Alcohol and other intoxicants are eminently suitable means of concealment. The FALSE SELF also builds a limited inner world: ways of thinking, views and opinions, and intellectual attitudes full of anxiety about otherness. An individual who is completely restricted to a "correct way of thinking" builds a sort of intellectual cult in her head in order to conceal herself from other people. The FALSE SELF draws the intellect into a fantasy world. The individual spends more time daydreaming than she does in real relationships and events.

Another response to anxiety is aggression.[23] If you have a person behaving aggressively and being violent (emotionally, verbally, and/or physically) around you, it is important to know that this person is afraid. If you happen to behave aggressively, and are honest with yourself, you will uncover anxiety behind every instance of your own aggressive behavior. **It is the scared person who goes on the attack**. A big strong dog does not even have to bark. It is the timorous little cur that tugs at your pant leg.

> *Most commonly, there is a combination of withdrawal and aggression. One man who came to us for help was more involved in politics and religion than most. He had long been staunchly committed to defending "values" and was a well-known Catholic activist. He came to us reluctantly, and only at the insistence of his wife, who had threatened to leave him unless he sought treatment. As it turned out, our patient had been having panic attacks and bouts of depression for years. Worst of all, however, was the violence to which he subjected those closest to him. He was very demanding on his children and not infrequently beat them. In a fit of rage, he once even went so far as to inflict verbal and physical violence on his wife as well. All this was diligently covered up, as it did not fit the image he had built around himself. When his wife had had enough and threatened to leave (and thereby cause a scandal),*

[23.]We distinguish between feeling angry and aggressive. Anger on its own is a morally neutral and beneficial **emotion**. When experienced in a disorderly manner, anger can lead to aggression, by which is meant morally reprehensible **activity** that causes harm to oneself and others.

he decided to come to our office and begrudgingly admitted to his problems.

It turned out that his behavior could be explained by having suffered a great deal of shame and anxiety in childhood. He lived with his parents in a small village, where his father was a notorious brawler and drunkard. Our patient, along with his mother and siblings, frequently ran away from home. His father beat him and never gave him any support. He told us that as a boy growing up, he was determined that he would never be like his father. That his own family arrangement actually became a carbon copy of his father's, except that he was an ardent teetotaller, was a bitter paradox. Fear and anxiety manifested themselves in him strongly, but he could not accept that he had those emotions and did everything possible to be rid of them.

Our patient decided to embark on the long road of therapy and spiritual development that lay before him. His transformation was effected amid tears and pain (literally: he began to cry for the first time in his adult life), and gradually found its expression in being increasingly more gentle towards himself, his "world" and those dear to him. The anxiety and depression attacks subsided, and the man abandoned his political activities, as he realized that the party he had been involved with was largely comprised of people like himself, frightened and aggressive.

These two defense mechanisms that people adopt might differ radically, but they have comparable wounds at their bases. Just as we have a positive and negative image of a photograph, these two kinds of attitudes and behaviors (namely the sad and the cheerful) can be traced back to the FALSE SELF.[24]

The sad version of the FALSE SELF involves living in isolation from other people, feeling worthless and remaining convinced of

---

[24] We are obviously deploying a schema that enables a certain general principle to be understood, but which risks oversimplifying matters. A "mixture" of the sad and happy versions of the FALSE SELF is usually encountered in practice.

being "not quite right," feeling unattractive, unintelligent, lacking perspective, not being needed by anyone, and so on. We have labelled this variety "sad" because sadness and a depressed mood come to the fore. Someone in this version of the FALSE SELF does not take up any challenges for fear of failure or form any relationships for fear of rejection. She is convinced that she will never succeed at anything in life and that nobody loves her.

The second version on the other hand is cheerful, but cheerful does not mean happy, because while the individual gives the impression of being happy, her cheerful behavior is the result of a defense mechanism having been activated.[25] In this variation, the individual can exhibit a great deal of scrappiness, is often boisterous, usually the life and soul of the party, and not infrequently successful (in politics, culture, the media, business, and even church organizations). As with the sad variation, however, she does not accept herself for who she is. This unconscious self-rejection drives all the activities the FALSE SELF deploys in its attempts to demonstrate its importance and value. These people sometimes build careers and go on to become "celebrities."

The sad FALSE SELF is less pleasant than the cheerful version. Paradoxically, therefore, it offers more opportunities for change than the cheerful version. Someone who has achieved "success" may not notice that he has been trapped for years.

It does not take an exceptionally well-trained eye to see that the behavior of certain politicians, journalists, stage people, and even church figures, indicates that their extraordinarily successful demeanour masks some deep-seated complexes. The price that has to be paid to maintain such an extravagant FALSE SELF is very high, but we do not see that paraded in front of the cameras. Their

---

[25] It is here worth noting that the word "gay" originally meant "cheerful" or "happy." This is symptomatic, as the "gay lifestyle" originates in the FALSE SELF.

laidback behavior is a cover for their fear of rejection. A careful observer, however, can spot the aggression that escapes these celebrities every so often. It is sad to watch one FALSE SELF doing a talk show with another FALSE SELF in the evening for the benefit of hundreds of thousands of other FALSE SELVES dreaming of a better life.

Defense mechanisms prevent true love. At most, the FALSE SELF can counterfeit love, so that if the individual remains on this level, she will be capable of a better or worse imitation. Whereas true love is completely unconditional, what we get from the FALSE SELF is an immature form of it in the form of a "commercial transaction."

> THE FALSE SELF LOVES IN ORDER TO GET SOMETHING OR AS A REWARD FOR SOMETHING – AND ONLY UNTIL A SUBJECTIVE, SELFISH ADVANTAGE IS ACHIEVED.

We are therefore dealing with imitations of love in the form of "hanging onto" someone (this version of the FALSE SELF gives rise to feelings of jealousy that are pathological, verging on paranoid) or of constantly purchasing affection (this version leads to a lack of assertiveness and a peculiar kind of emotional prostitution: "if only they loved me.") When the FALSE SELF has to transcend itself and enter into true love, which is never without of an element of sacrifice, it retreats and shuts itself away, scurrying off into seclusion.

IV.

SELF-ESTEEM

We often hear that someone "has low self-esteem" and needs to work on it. We hear that someone has raised his self-esteem through therapy, or conversely, that someone's self-esteem has plummeted, perhaps after failing an exam. But are these descriptions accurate or appropriate? Can self-esteem wax and wane?

In our view, such is not the case. We have found from working with people that just as a woman cannot be more or less pregnant, the terms high or low self-esteem are not really appropriate.

> SELF-ESTEEM
> IS AN EITHER/OR THING:
> EITHER I'M IN TOUCH WITH MY SELF-
> WORTH (LIVING IN THE REAL SELF), OR
> I'M NOT (LIVING IN THE FALSE SELF).

We also consider descriptions of the "building of self-esteem" to be invalid. Obviously, someone functioning within the confines of the FALSE SELF is not in touch with his self-worth, and therefore has to "build" it somehow. This "structure," however, is as flimsy as a house built on sand. Even a palace or a bunker can be built on shaky foundations (and some people actually function like this), but they will never last due to the weakness of the base (the FALSE SELF). **There is no need to build anything on the REAL SELF. The individual simply gets in touch with his self-worth. On this level, we can see that our worth is infinite, as it results from nothing less than**

an act of creation by God, who wants us for who we are. The individual who lives in awareness of this truth does not need anyone to vindicate his worth. That is because it is continually being affirmed internally by the Love that created it.

The worth of an individual can neither be increased nor decreased. Nor is there any need to work on it. The individual can be in touch with his self-worth, or not. In the same way that gold remains gold regardless of whether it is found on a finger or in the mud, an individual can live with the experience of his beauty, and consistent with his calling. Then again, he may be completely unaware of his worth. This often leads to a life that is not worthy of him. We cannot produce gold; we have to search for it.[26] Each of us has an invaluable metal inside, but not everyone can tap into it.

When it comes to accessing our self-worth, progress is not linear, but consists in "leaping" from the FALSE SELF to the REAL SELF ("from sand to rock, from sand to rock", etc.). Some people live exclusively in the FALSE SELF and bringing them into the real world can take a long time. We initially have to deal with brief instances of contact with reality. These only last a few seconds or a couple of minutes. If, however, the individual is determined, he can function in the REAL SELF increasingly more often. He is then fully in touch with his self-worth. He sometimes manages to stay in this state for a couple of days. External difficulties, however, can very quickly catapult him back to the FALSE SELF, as this false defensive identity is instinctive and reflexive, and is activated whenever a threat is detected. What we have, then, is a standard "leaping" situation: FALSE SELF – REAL SELF; either one or the other; there is no halfway.

---

[26] Gold can be made from mercury inside nuclear reactors and cyclotrons. This, however, is not profitable.

If we wanted to depict this graphically, it would appear as follows:

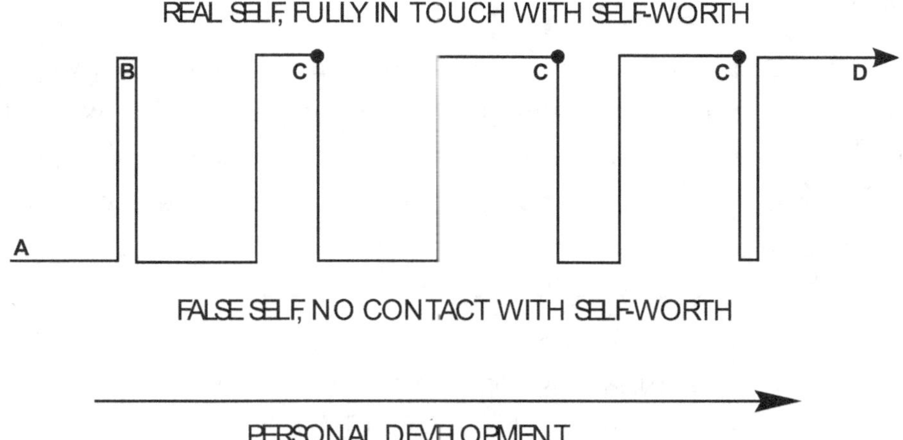

We develop by gradually moving away from functioning in the FALSE SELF ("A") and towards functioning in the REAL SELF ("D"). At first we only get in touch with our self-worth for a few moments, if at all ("B"). As we develop, we gradually approach the reverse situation, where we function in the REAL SELF most of the time (fully in touch with our self-worth).

We would like to focus on the moments marked "C." These are of special interest, as they precede the "collapse of the FALSE SELF. The "just before" moment ("C"), which precedes its being supplanted by the REAL SELF, is most often an incident that evokes some childhood hurt and triggers a reflexive fight-or-flight response. This will sometimes be very subtle, for example, an innocent gesture, an association, or a fragrance wafting in the air, so the sensations will be almost subliminal, although it can almost always be detected. We are especially interested in analyzing the "C" moments, as it is on these that our self-development should be focused.

Growth leads the individual to find his REAL SELF. This is what the individual needs to adopt and sometimes even build his life on almost from the outset.

We need to spend some time now on affirmation. If our worth does not depend on anything external, then **affirmation will not build our self-esteem**. We know, however, that an unloved, unaffirmed individual will not grow properly. What role, then does affirmation play?

AFFIRMATION CREATES THE CONDITIONS FOR AN INDIVIDUAL TO BE ABLE TO GET IN TOUCH WITH HIS SELF-WORTH (AND RETURN TO THE REAL SELF), BUT IT DOES NOT GUARANTEE THIS IN AND OF ITSELF.

Affirmation reduces anxiety, and so defense mechanisms can be dropped more readily. The younger the individual, the more important the role of affirmation. For this reason, children feel its absence very keenly. Affirmation makes the individual feel temporarily better, thereby creating a favorable setting for self-development. Getting back to the REAL SELF, however, is always associated with effort.

We remember meeting a 25-year-old woman who complained that those around her (her family, friends, and community) did not understand her and failed to meet her needs and expectations. She was morbidly obese and addicted to food, but she never raised that issue. The problem was other people.

After speaking further with her, it transpired that her resentments had no rational foundation. Things that were trivial to an outside observer triggered powerful emotional agitation and opposition in her. We obviously did not tell her as much, as that was likely to be the end of her coming to us. Being cognizant that nobody chooses the things that hurt them, we treated her with a great deal of warmth and respect. Several sessions ensued in this sort of understanding atmosphere. However, as soon as we gently began to suggest that she had something to work on, she reacted very nervously and stopped coming to us, claiming that we did not understand her.

We sometimes meet people who are treated with a great deal of kindness and who frequently hear words of love. They are loved by those around them in a wise and appropriate manner, but their condition does not improve. This is because affirmation does not do the internal work involved in finding the REAL SELF for anybody.[27] It might create more favorable conditions for growth, but it is no substitute for self-development. That is something that everyone has to undertake on their own.

The genuine nature of what is commonly called "low self-esteem" should be recognized. We have already said that an individual out of touch with his self-worth (that is, with the REAL SELF) uses defense mechanisms to create a false identity that is meant to imitate the REAL SELF. We have also said that we were made to love, and that consistent development in collaboration with grace leads to deification. As our nature has as its inborn goal to participate in the interior life of God, the FALSE SELF will also have "divine aspirations," but they will be realized in their own false way.

It is sometimes thought that a person with low self-esteem will struggle to raise his own personal bar to a height that most people could clear without difficulty. What we have in mind here is a kind of virtual national average of appearance, education, interpersonal skills, and other human endowments and abilities. One might think an appropriate prop might enable such a person to eventually clear

---

[27] In the theological scheme of things, God's respect for the freedom of the individual is likewise expressed in this manner: "Follow me if you wish." Grace requires our consent at each stage of development.

this bar and to make his problems go away. It quickly turns out, however, that after achieving whichever goal a positive state of mind was supposedly hinging on, such a person quickly reverts to complaining. His good mood lasts only a short while. This confirms that **the real problem of people with so-called low-self-esteem lies in wanting to be like God**. And because they cannot achieve this, they become frustrated, and cancel many activities and sever many relationships.

If you have ever met a very chic woman who sees herself as ugly and is always after something to improve her appearance, or someone who has graduated with several degrees, but still deems himself incapable of doing anything, then you will know where we are coming from. **A person with low self-esteem will never be satisfied with himself, even if he achieves results that are, objectively speaking, above-average.**

The FALSE SELF has divine aspirations and raises the requirement bar to an impossible height that cannot be cleared. Four major internal necessities to which someone afflicted with low self-esteem succumbs, can be distinguished. Think of these as four ways such people feel the need to be a god.

"THE DIVINE ASPIRATIONS" OF THE
FALSE SELF:

1. EVERYTHING HAS TO GO RIGHT FOR ME.
2. EVERYONE SHOULD LOVE AND RESPECT ME.
3. EVERYTHING SHOULD TURN OUT THE WAY I WANT.
4. EVERYONE SHOULD DO AND THINK AS I DO.

---

1. EVERYTHING HAS TO GO RIGHT FOR ME

Someone constrained by needing everything going right for him will experience those horrible moments when something goes wrong. Obviously, we "mere mortals" also want everything to go right, but we are only too aware that this does not always happen. But, alas, we are only "mere mortals." It is different with the "gods." Everything always has to go right for them. If, then, an individual with divine aspirations has something not go right -- if he has to face the fact that he is no god -- he falls from a very great height and shatters. He falls into melancholy, and even despair, experiences enormous frustration, and stops doing anything. The FALSE SELF is not equipped to cope with failure. We "mere mortals" are not exactly overjoyed when something does not go our way either, but at least we accept that things can and do go wrong. We try again. **For the FALSE SELF, failure is something to be abhorred**.

We know people who are almost panic-stricken by the thought that something might not work out and who turn to therapeutic help. The prospect of private therapy sessions arouses tremendous fear in them. After all, word might get around that they are in therapy. We understand that those who come to us have an obvious need for privacy, but this sort of intense fear exposes the need of the FALSE SELF to remain a god, namely, this thinking that nobody can find out that I have problems, as gods are not supposed to have problems.

We remember one particular young man whose father had rejected him in childhood and who had a morbid terror of failing at anything in any field. His life was being constricted by shame. After a breakthrough in therapy, he sensibly decided to tell a few of his friends that he was getting psychological help. He was surprised to find that his workmates not only did not laugh at him or reject him, but on the contrary, expressed their support and showed respect. He was even more surprised when some of them asked for our number.

THE FALSE SELF manages to continuously vie with others. It competes and compares itself: "Am I good enough?" This makes people with "low self-esteem" withdraw from a lot of life activities. When someone has aspirations to be a god, he has to be the best.

2. EVERYONE SHOULD LOVE AND RESPECT ME

Someone who has this "divine necessity" to be loved, praised, and respected by everybody will be mortified whenever confronted with aversion, or even mild criticism. **The FALSE SELF finds it unbearable that someone might not like something about him**. We "mere mortals" know all too well that the person liked by everyone has yet to be born. This is why we can take criticism. This is why our appearance does not have to be perfect. This is why we can live with bodily defects. We can stammer in public, admit to mistakes, have a stain on our pants, and so forth. But, alas, we are "mere mortals." It is by no means pleasant when someone has something against us, but that is just life. Only someone who has never done anything has never made a mistake, and is therefore immune to criticism. But it is a completely different story for the gods. They have to be perfect, because they need to be treated with an almost godlike reverence. It is strictly forbidden to criticize them or joke about them. Forgetting their names will bring about the end of the world. They almost break down if someone important to them singles out someone else (by smiling at her, inviting her to dance, or talking to her at a party), as this means that they are being treated on a par with others, whereas their FALSE SELF craves to be a god, and requires adoration befitting a god. When this adoration is not forthcoming, the "low-self-esteem" person feels deeply wounded and vows never again to take a risk. He severs the relationship and/or tries to destroy whoever it was who criticized him. This often happens unwittingly. The FALSE SELF reasons that "if that's how things are, then it's not worth keeping this relationship," and makes sure not to stray outside the region in which his godlike status is assured.

One person was mortally offended when she was asked to step aside a few feet, as she was obstructing something on the blackboard behind her. Another severed her relationships with several acquaintances, because. according to her, they had been ridiculing her in their conversations. Nobody could tell exactly what it was all about - probably some innocent joke she found unacceptable. **This shows that jokes, while necessary and possible, should only be made about oneself. You can ever tell what is going on inside the other person.**

3. EVERYTHING SHOULD TURN OUT THE WAY I WANT

It is disastrous for someone with this need to be a god, this need to have everything turn out his way, to have something not go as expected. And anything might not go as expected - it could rain during your vacation, your flight could be delayed, you could get a flat tire, or someone might snatch up that last great bargain before you. You can also get sick, grow old, and even die, as unlikely as this last contingency seems to some. Alas, these things happen to "mere mortals." We know that life is hard and that we just have to cope somehow. We are certainly not indifferent to hardship and we sometimes worry for all sorts of reasons. But as miserable as this makes us, we endure it, for such is the lot of humankind.

Not so for the gods. Every setback is the end of the world. A fall from their Olympian heights leads to the astounding revelation that they are only human. For many gods, this is not to be borne. They became sad and frustrated, and can fall into depression. They lose the will to live. The FALSE SELF would like to transfer its false life to eternity, but cannot do so.

4. EVERYONE SHOULD THINK AND ACT AS I DO

The fourth necessity is a "desire that everybody think and act as I do." This necessity is arguably the most godlike, as it means nothing less than creating a fellow human being in our own image.[28] This may well be the most prevalent "divine necessity" in our native land of Poland. It is enough to listen to Poles discussing politics in the evening. Here are the longings of the FALSE SELF: "To take possession of the other person, have him completely to myself, make him only interested in me, get him to think only what I deem correct, have him only behave in a manner acceptable to me, and get him to share my political views, which are obviously the most best and most equitable." Are you familiar with this despotic way of thinking? Pathological jealousy and ambition stem from this need to be god. It can even lead to outbursts of rage at people who think differently, have different views, or look or behave differently. **The "divine" FALSE SELF aims to have everyone focus on him, and to reshape the world according to his vision. When he does not succeed, he becomes frustrated, cuts himself off, and frequently goes on the attack. Most perpetrators of violence are undervalued people.**

People with "low self-esteem" have extremely high expectations of themselves, higher than the average person, and when they cannot clear it, they fall apart. When we get these people in the office, we sit them down, and once we've explained the root cause of the problem, we walk around them and jokingly recite the liturgical hymn Glory to God in the Highest: "We praise you, we bless you, we adore you, we glorify you." And you know what? Some of them can't stand it. They cry out "Enough! No more! Please stop!" and immediately spring out of the chair. Others smile blissfully, and when we ask them what they're feeling, they answer with extraordinary sincerity: "Great!" They laugh heartily and don't even

---

[28.] The Bible states that this is how God created us (cf. Gen. 1:26-27).

try to feign embarrassment. Have you ever thought about "low self-esteem" that way?

A good FALSE SELF test is to ask the person with "low-self-esteem" if they are average in any area. As incredible as it sounds, some of them almost have panic attacks at the thought of being average. Strange, isn't it? On the one hand, they claim that they are "nothing" and "worthless," but on the other, they sink into despair on hearing that they might simply be average. This exposes the true nature of what is commonly called low self-esteem: it is hubris, or arrogance and pride.

There is yet another important aspect to consider. A certain paradox can be seen in all those seated upon this "divine throne" and looking down on others. They supposedly feel inferior, but yet they are very quick to judge others, and their verdicts are extraordinarily severe. They often despise others, trust no one, and believe that people are bad. Their attitude towards their fellow human beings is seemingly at odds with their appraisal of themselves as being of little worth. If they accepted their own weaknesses, they would be more charitable towards others. However, as pseudo-gods, they lay claim to the right to harshly judge and criticize others "from on high."

The issues discussed here lie on the boundary between psychology and spirituality. If we observe the workings of Jesus from a psychological perspective, we can see that he challenged people to abandon the FALSE SELF and seek out the REAL SELF. His "Whoever seeks to preserve his life will lose it..."[29] and "... Unless a grain of wheat falls to the ground and dies, it remains just a grain of wheat..."[30] can be paraphrased as "Whoever wants to keep the FALSE SELF will lose the REAL SELF" and "You will not be capable of love until the FALSE SELF dies." The parable about

---

[29] Luke 17:33.

[30] John 12:24.

building on sand as opposed to rock illustrates the choice of how to live: will you build on the FALSE SELF, or will you rely on our own true worth, which comes from God?

There is an oft-quoted phrase from St. Paul that can also be interpreted in this light: "… yet I live; no longer I (that is, the FALSE SELF) but Christ lives in me…".[31] Well, are you not surprised? The disintegration of the FALSE SELF opens us up to receive grace. Once the counterfeit life has disintegrated, nothing stands in the way of deification, or union with God. The FALSE SELF, however, must be completely annihilated before we can experience this.

> **THE REAL SELF** IS POTENTIAL STORAGE
> CAPACITY FOR GRACE.

When this structure, which attempts to imitate the divine, collapses and the individual finally abandons all the defense mechanisms that separate him from himself, from people, and from the Creator, he will be able to love with a pure love that has its source in God Himself. After this collapse, Adam will come out of the garden without having to dress in any loincloth to hide his nakedness.[32] Owning up to his own weakness will allow him to again find himself in the arms of the Father, where he will also discover his own beauty and value. The road to Christian sanctity relies on being so open to grace that one becomes Christ through participation in the divine life[33]. The Catechism of the Catholic Church, citing some wonderful texts, states that **God became human so that humans**

---

[31] Cf. Gal. 2:20.

[32] Cf. Gen. 3:9-11.

[33] 2 Pet. 1:4.

could become God.[34] The breathtaking goal of our development is thus uncovered for us.

Here, we would like to refer to some very similar expressions used in the New Age. The depth psychology of Carl Jung, as well as the other "spiritual" trends that encapsulate the New Age mindset, stress that the individual possesses a certain "divine potential" that he should discover within himself. The New Age is not concerned with philosophical coherence and so cherry-picks from psychology and various religious traditions (including Christianity), thereby aping genuine psychology and spirituality. The currents of thought associated with the New Age maintain that the individual is supposed to discover his divinity by drawing on a range of disparate techniques (i.e. self-salvation), whereas Christianity challenges him to work together with the grace that he receives freely from God (i.e. to accept salvation). This working together consists of faith, prayer, asceticism, and love of our fellow human beings. The individual is not a "dormant" god, but a creation. **The individual does not discover his divinity, but can receive the grace that will deify him.**

It can be safely asserted that the New Age proclaims the emancipation of the individual, invites him to build a sophisticated temple of the FALSE SELF, and in so doing, paradoxically enslaves him to himself. The difference between the New Age and Christian comprehension of development is fundamental, but at the same time, very subtle, in this respect. Unfortunately, Christians often do not notice this and are either seduced by the New Age, or conversely, in their desire to keep faith with sound teaching, reject the very crux of Christian spirituality (the perspective of the deification of the individual in the contemplative way). The answer

---

[34] Catechism of the Catholic Church, Paragraph 460: The Word became flesh to make us "partakers of the divine nature": "For this is why the Word became man, and the Son of God became the Son of man: so that man, by entering into communion with the Word and thus receiving divine sonship, might become a son of God." "For the Son of God became man so that we might become God." "The only-begotten Son of God, wanting to make us sharers in his divinity, assumed our nature, so that he, made man, might make men gods."

to these errors may be the Christian concept of personal growth, which is partly described in our book.

We call the therapeutic approach we have devised Integral Christian Therapy (ICT). We use a variety of techniques, not to give anyone the illusion of divinity, but so that by understanding himself, a person can stand before God and ask to be healed (that is, to receive salvation). Although emancipation comes from God, it is only fair that we do everything humanly possible to open ourselves up to it. As Joan of Arc is said to have put it: "We must fight for God to give victory." Working on ourselves is therefore of fundamental importance in ICT.

As we have already stated, love is only possible with the REAL SELF. Only then are we in touch with our self-worth, which is infinite and does not require building or defending. Moreover, a relationship with God is only possible with the REAL SELF. We discover that God does not reject us on account of our infirmity. On the contrary, it is precisely our infirmity that summons His merciful love. We gradually begin to open ourselves up to grace. The road of humbly accepting ourselves thereby becomes the road to union with God.

We have access to infinity through the REAL SELF. We can say, using contemporary imagery, that the REAL SELF is like a gateway through which we can enter eternity while still living in time. **Whoever has access to the REAL SELF is liberated from external circumstances and from himself, as he is not forced to put on any masks. He discovers life in himself**[35] and is therefore not dependent on public opinion, the state of the economy, or anything else. He does not have to chase popularity or seek fame and fortune. Nor is he excessively concerned about his health. He obviously has difficulties, but they cannot take his life away, because he knows that

---

[35]·Cf. John 5:26.

the source of life, that is, God, resides within him. The freedom thereby gained becomes a springboard for love and duty. Having discovered his value, identity, dignity, and beauty, the individual begins to live with an abundance of aptitudes and abilities which he develops, and in so doing, makes the world yield to him.[36] He is committed to serving the human family in his social, political, economic, and cultural life.

> THE COEXISTENCE OF RESOLVE AND GENTLENESS IS THE SIGN OF LIVING IN THE REAL SELF.

[36.]Cf. Gen 1:28.

PART II

"SELF-DEVELOPMENT"

I.

KNOWING ONESELF

"Self-knowledge is necessary in order to extract everything from the subconscious, so that everything is clear and simple." Some might ascribe these words to a famous psychoanalyst, but the author was anything but that. This advice came from a young priest named Karol Wojtyła.[37] In fact, inner growth requires you to know yourself and accept the truth about yourself. This is known as "recognizing" with humility in theology, and "insight" in psychology.

There is a certain battle to fight if we want to grow and develop. Our adversary lies hidden before us. She wants to take us by surprise and attack while remaining hidden, like a guerrilla. This adversary is the FALSE SELF and we will have to learn her strategy if we are going to defeat her. We need to know the structure of the brokenness we carry within us, if we are to pick the most effective preventive measures. Getting to the truth about ourselves takes determination, courage, and the intellectual flexibility to listen to difficult things and adopt ways of thinking different from those we have regarded as natural and proper for years. When Jesus began his ministry he declared "Repent, and believe the gospel.[38]" In the original Greek, this sentence more clearly reads: "Change your

---

[37] Wanda Półtawska, *Beskidzkie rekolekcje. Dzieje przyjaźni księdza Karola Wojtyły z rodziną Półtawskich [Memories of the Beskidy Hills: The Story of the Friendship between Fr. Karol Wojtyła and the Półtawski Family]*, Edycja Świętego Pawła, 27 February 2009, p. 48.

[38] Mark 1:15.

thinking and believe the gospel." Experience shows that very few people are prepared to change their thinking.

Simply knowing oneself is extraordinary liberating. When Karol Wojtyła, as Pope John Paul II, was asked which Biblical verse was most important to him, he answered, quoting the Gospel of John: **"And you will know the truth, and the truth will set you free.**[39]**"** This is precisely what we are talking about. By knowing the composition of the FALSE SELF, we can begin to catch those thoughts, attitudes, actions, and judgments that are defense mechanisms that detach us from reality. It can be a shock to realize that almost every direction in our life has drawn its inspiration from the FALSE SELF. Reclaiming "internal independence" costs a great deal of pain, but pain loses its importance in the face of the joy of regaining the self.[40]

> INSIGHT IS USUALLY UNPLEASANT, AND EVEN HIGHLY UNPLEASANT, IN THE BEGINNING.

Instinctively and sometimes vehemently denying what we begin to see is, likewise, very typical. The eye is constructed in such a way that the entire retina is covered by photosensitive cone and rod cells. The retina, however has a blind spot. This can easily be demonstrated through optic experimentation.[41] Although the blind spot is near the center of the retina, we are unaware of its existence because the other eye compensates for the missing image portion. **The brain cannot see that it does not see**. We are similarly blind to

---

[39] John 8:32.

[40] The first part of the "Matrix" trilogy has a painful scene where the hero is disconnected from the fake, virtual world in which he has unknowingly been living.

[41] The blind spot is the place where there are no cone or rod cells. This is where the optic nerve goes from the retina to the brain.

our own defense mechanisms. (Recall that they initially played a positive role.) Disassembling them will bring about spontaneous peace, because the places where we've been hurt are laid bare. And it can be said with absolute certainty that **the first and most important emotional response to learning the truth about ourselves is fear, occasionally coupled with sadness and/or anger**. The FALSE SELF does what it can to protect itself. We prefer not to see, hear, or understand, or we disown something patently obvious to an outside observer. We place the problem outside ourselves, and prefer to change the whole world than tackle the difficulty.

How many of us say "He annoys me," instead of stating "I'm annoyed with him"? This is not mere word play. If the cause of my annoyance is external, then I should eliminate it. On the other hand, if I acknowledge that I am responsible for being annoyed by someone, I can ask what it is **within me** that allows someone to annoy me. In this way, I can recognize that **there is a problem within me** as well.[42] Fear makes its entrance at this very moment. "Won't I be hurt again, and in the same place as before, if I admit to a weakness and reveal it?" A mechanism that we define as "Full speed astern![43]" comes into play. It is **anxiety that does not let us see the composition of the FALSE SELF.**

We should further add that there are people who always find fault with themselves and are prepared to admit to any accusation. However, we should not let ourselves be deceived. This attitude is not a sign of humility, but fear manifested by withdrawal instead of aggression. This constant self-blame is yet another defense mechanism emanating from the FALSE SELF. There is an enormous

---

[42.]This is not to say that someone who annoys us does not need to change either. However, we are only interested in ourselves (in the positive sense of that phrase) for now. We cannot effectively influence another person other than by modifying our own attitudes and behaviour. We always have to begin with ourselves. Our impact on others will always be very limited.

[43.]That is, backwards.

difference between the humility of St. Peter and the despair of Judas. **Both betrayed their friend, but they responded to their betrayal differently**. With Peter, humility prevailed; with Judas, despair. Judas is not the epitome of a humble person in hanging himself. He (his FALSE SELF) was unable to bear the truth about himself.

> ACQUIRING INSIGHT REQUIRES ANOTHER PERSON.

We need a mirror when we have something on our face, as we cannot see it ourselves. Another person can serve as this mirror. **If there were no people around, it might seem that we loved the whole world**. However, we receive information about what we are interiorly every day, and this information is quite often unpleasant. If we courageously take up the challenge, we soon realize that the more difficult the relationship, situation, or contact with someone else, the more we can learn about what we are interiorly. **People who hurt us, annoy us, and shatter our sense of well-being are therefore especially valuable**. They can be facetiously described as our secret allies. Examples of this are therapists who have the deepest and most incisive insights, and retreats run by those whom God has sent to show us the sickness in our hearts. But do we want to listen to what is brought up in such ways? After all, most of us avoid difficult people and situations. Nobody likes to be hurt or offended. Most people do anything to avoid confronting a disagreeable person or situation, but by so doing, they rob themselves of an opportunity for personal growth. Obviously, this is not about engaging in some sort of masochism, but asking ourselves whether we really want to obtain the insight that difficult people and situations have to offer, and whether we want to learn something about the FALSE SELF. Don't we almost automatically think "the other person" is the one with the problem and that we do not need to change anything about ourselves?

Until we respond to the person who has hurt us with merciful love and understanding,[44] until we respond to a situation of "being jolted out of our sense of well-being" with calm and leniency, we will always have something that remains to be done and there will always remain a framework within us waiting to be broken down. **Anything that thwarts[45] our plans is like an ultrasound probe that God applies to our heart**, so that we can see its condition. We see whether the sickness has been cured, or whether it is seriously threatening our life by spreading silently and insidiously.

Many people seem willing to approach difficulties in life in precisely this way. We recall a man who, when told that his X-ray revealed a tumour, angrily tore up the negative and broke off contact with the doctor, as he refused to accept this painful information. The emotions that are involuntarily aroused in situations we find difficult are an immense gift here. We can kid ourselves that love is within us until these kinds of emotional responses that are impossible to ignore, are aroused within us. We shall now briefly consider this.

---

[44] This does not by any means give us the right to lay down restrictions and requirements.

[45] The phrase "thwarting plans" is a beautiful play on words in Polish, as the word for "thwarting" (pokrzyżowanie) contains the word "cross" (krzyż). As such, it can denote setbacks and allude to Christian spirituality, where the cross is the road to salvation.

II.

FEELINGS

Although clinical understanding of emotional phenomena is constantly expanding, some people still understand feelings as divisible into two categories: positive or negative feelings. This often goes in tandem with ascribing considerable moral significance to them: sinful and unacceptable feelings vs. moral and acceptable feelings. It sometimes happens that feelings which are pleasant experiences, such as joy, peace, and love, are considered positive, while those that are unpleasant to experience such as anger, envy, and fear are considered negative. We also occasionally encounter the view that certain feelings are harmful to their owner.

> FEELINGS ARE NEITHER POSITIVE NOR NEGATIVE. FEELINGS DO NOT HAVE MORAL VALUE. ACTS COMMITTED UNDER THE IMPACT OF FEELINGS HAVE MORAL SIGNIFICANCE.

If one of our clients insists on this division, we ask him to name a feeling which he considers "positive."

Take joy as an example. A heroin addict feels joy in getting a guaranteed daily supply of the drug. Or, consider that love is felt by someone going to his lover. And perhaps there would be nothing wrong with that, were it not that she has a husband and three children, and he is a priest with a vow of celibacy. In this way, so-called positive feelings somehow cease to be positive.

What about anger, jealousy, and fear? Aren't some of these feelings, which we categorize as negative, listed among the deadly sins in Scripture? How then should they be treated?

Consider anger for a moment. If it was a sin to be angry, then how do we explain the scene, described in the gospel of Mark, where Jesus was angry?[46] And jealousy? Haven't you heard about the "jealousy of the Lord of Hosts"? And fear? Wouldn't you be afraid whenever your life and health were endangered?

It is crucially important to us that our clients understand that all feelings, even those commonly regarded as unpleasant, have an important function to perform. Anger, for instance, is a personal growth engine and is essential for maintaining relationships. Contrary to the conventional view, if anger never surfaces in a relationship, this is very often a sign of a nearly dead relationship rather than a sign of unity. Anger gives life force, and enables boundaries to be set and values defended. Jealousy can likewise inspire us to grow and to affirm the achievements of others. An opinion expressed under the influence of jealousy properly experienced, such as, "I envy your achievements. You must have worked really hard. I'd like to achieve something similar myself in the future," sounds really beautiful, and expresses admiration and respect for someone's work. Many people handle their sexual emotions disastrously. They do not rejoice in them, but treat them as something bad or immoral, as if God had made a mistake in endowing people with them.[47] Our so-called negative feelings are

---

[46] Again he entered the synagogue. There was a man there who had a withered hand. They watched him closely to see if he would cure him on the Sabbath so that they might accuse him. He said to the man with the withered hand, "Come up here before us." Then he said to them, "Is it lawful to do good on the Sabbath rather than to do evil, to save life rather than to destroy it?" But they remained silent. **Looking around at them with anger** and grieved at their hardness of heart, he said to the man, "Stretch out your hand." He stretched it out and his hand was restored. (Mark 3:1-5).

[47] As surprising as this may be to some, even homosexual feelings have their own positive role to fulfil for those who experience them and they by no means have to lead to homosexual acts. They should therefore not be suppressed. We shall not expand on this topic further.

sadly so often misunderstood by those who experience them and fail to accept them.

One of the most important roles they play in our emotional lives is communication.

FEELINGS PUT US IN TOUCH WITH THE OUTER WORLD, WITH OTHER PEOPLE, WITH OURSELVES, AND WITH GOD.

We do not realize how much information comes to us through emotional channels. Even inanimate nature is received by us emotionally. We obviously communicate with another person by expressing and receiving emotions. It is similar with prayer. If prayer is meant to be wholly human and Christian, then it will be accompanied by our feelings. Meeting a "person" as fascinating as God is always reflected in our emotional nature. Note that the words "**communi**on" and "**communi**cation" have the same etymology. This fact alone reveals something important, namely, that there can be no communion without communication. Love, or communion, ceases to be possible when the emotional sphere does not function properly.

The reason that many religious people suppress their emotional nature is that they interpret certain feelings generated within them as sinful or unchristian. This calls to mind a certain young man who was "cultivating" a serious anxiety neurosis. It all began when he received a First Holy Communion prayer book from his religious instructor. The examination of conscience in this book read something like: "Have you ever been angry with your Mom? Have you ever been angry with your Dad? Have you ever been irritated by a teacher?" and so on. The cited questions clearly have to do with feelings regarded as sinful. Our client's unhappiness consisted in being overly concerned with this examination of conscience, and doing whatever he could to avoid feeling anger and irritation. Until he reached adulthood, he based his preparations for confessing his sins on a book that he had been given when he was eight. His suppressed feelings of assertiveness were then supplanted by fear. It did not take much for obsessions to make their presence felt.

Parents can sometimes unwittingly contribute to their children developing the emotional problems that go with suppressed feelings. Children may begin to suppress feelings of anger, pain, sadness, and fear when their parents, for whatever reason, will not let them be expressed. We should not try to persuade a child who falls down and cries that "it doesn't hurt anymore," even if we really wish he were not feeling pain. On the contrary, she should be allowed to cry and be hugged and have what she feels confirmed with understanding ("I know it hurts, it really hurts..."). **Children must be allowed to express their anger (in a socially acceptable manner), and not be frightened when curiosity about their bodies and sexual feelings are aroused**. Suppressed feelings can also result from a negative experience if the adults in the child's environment, under the influence of anger (for example) have done bad things. This will leave the false conviction that anger is invariably associated with violence.

Some people try to erase their emotional nature as an unnecessary or even harmful comain. They suppress their feelings because they were molested, made fun of, or rejected in childhood. Their emotional realm is full of pain, and the pain subsides when they do not permit themselves certain feelings. However, feelings cannot be selectively shut out to leave only those that are desired. Our emotional nature can be likened to an electronic keyboard instrument where the keyboard is the complete palette of feelings and each key is a single feeling. We cannot mute only one key. We either silence all of them or none of them. **To suppress anger or** sexual feelings is to yield to the suppression of the entire emotional domain. To be incapable of anger is to be incapable of love as well.

We have devoted a fair amount of space to this issue because we will never be able to recognize the composition of FALSE SELF unless we consciously work with our feelings. This is because **feelings commonly classified as negative are exactly the feelings that surface at the times most crucial for development**. It is vital to realize that our emotional nature not only puts us in contact with the outside world, but also with the inner one.

> FEELINGS CAN TELL US A LOT
> ABOUT OUR DEFENSE MECHANISMS.
> WE NEED TO LISTEN TO THEM AND
> UNDERSTAND THEIR LANGUAGE.

Our emotional nature is like echo sounding on a ship. Although the seabed is not normally visible, it contains hills and valleys, wrecks, shoals, and reefs. So long as they are invisible to a ship's captain, they all threaten navigational safety. Echo sounding enables him to detect things normally hidden beneath the surface of the water.

Human psychology works in a similar manner. Someone with a wounded heart has a fracture buried deep within him, which threatens catastrophe. It can only be detected by interpreting the waves that it sends up, and which resonate with certain external circumstances. These waves are our feelings, and it is through them that we receive information about our otherwise inaccessible interior. **Our feelings do not tell us what we must do, but inform us about what is going on inside us.** And they do not, as is commonly but erroneously believed, tell us about the outside world. Some, having experienced anger, are convinced that others are angry with them.

Whether we want one or not, our emotions are an independent jury that delivers a verdict on our inner selves. They are like a go-between who wants to deliver a message. In antiquity, a messenger who brought bad news was put to death – as if that could change anything about the news! But some of us treat or our own unwelcome feelings exactly the same way. Others allow the messenger to take command. That is also a mistake. The messenger must be heard. No more, no less. Once we understand that, we can stop working on our feelings (trying to modify them), and start to work with them by accepting whatever information they have to deliver.

It may happen that we fail to interpret our feelings correctly. We then need guidance, therapy, or at least a mature friendship. **A kind person, internally free enough not to hesitate to tell us painful things, is an invaluable gift on the path to personal growth.** In a sense, such a person is indispensable because **it is very difficult to evaluate oneself without external assistance**.

Understanding our own emotional states requires time and patience. The mind is not able to accurately interpret the feelings generated within us. I see someone for the first time and there is no way I can find out why this person arouses a mixture of anger and fear in me. He has done nothing to me, but I feel antipathy towards him and even want to attack him. Why is this happening? My mind doesn't yet know. It is a long time before it clicks that this man was wearing the same vest as the gym teacher who humiliated me in front of the entire class thirty years ago. My feelings had come to warn me: "Be careful – this person can hurt you because he's like that other one years ago." The understanding is there to gauge the credibility of the threat – and to decide whether to withdraw, defend yourself, or casually continue the conversation.

Some people, having felt something similar, have become aggressive towards a completely blameless "man in a vest." Others, feeling what they assess as unjustified anger towards their neighbor, immediately confess to God their sin of being "deficient in love."

Emotional independence makes mature love possible and is therefore worth reflecting on for a moment. **A fully autonomous person lives in touch with his own worth and functions in the REAL SELF**. An integrated and mature person adopts a mature attitude that avoids the extremes of excessive emotions towards people (being dependent on other people or vice versa) and independence (a defensive attitude leading to isolation and loneliness).[48]

> EMOTIONAL INDEPENDENCE IS ATTAINED WHEN THE EMOTIONAL SPHERE BECOMES FULLY INTEGRATED; WHEN THE EMOTIONAL LIFE IS COMPATIBLE WITH THE AGITATION OF THE WILL.
> EMOTIONAL INDEPENDENCE IS EXPRESSED BY HAVING RELATIONSHIPS PROPERLY "ADJUSTED" TO SURROUNDINGS.

Feelings allow us to gauge the extent to which we are independent. Let us demonstrate this with the use of an archetypal scene: The proverbial bum[49] is at a bus shelter. He is screaming

---

[48] Independence is currently promoted by the secular world as a virtue to strive after. It is worth emphasizing that independence is both an emotional and spiritual snare, because it hinders love and communion. A completely independent person does not love anybody, because love implies entering into dependence, which should not, however, be confused with a loss of freedom. The wedding rings we wear are not symbols of lost freedom, but tokens of how freedom has been realized. We remain free while being mutually dependent, in marriage.

[49] The word "bum" here denotes someone commonly regarded as being at the bottom of the social hierarchy, that is, someone whose opinion concerns us least.

abuse to someone on the other side of the street. Note the various possible reactions of a person on the receiving end of this vitriol. That person might cringe and think "Even the bum thinks I'm a loser," and then have a miserable day, sadly wondering why anyone would insult him like that. This person is our model for the lowest level of independence.

Or, the receiver might angrily shout back, or even go over and beat the bum up, in order to protect his own good name. This person is higher on our scale. Then again, he might feel superior and mutter something like "Piss off, you old fart," not arguing with the bum, but arrogantly ignoring him. This person is even higher on our scale, but still not on the top rung. Even more independent would be someone who, having been verbally attacked by a vagrant, looks at him with love and empathy, thinking "What sort of misery must that guy be in to behave like that?" He would not feel superior, contemptuous, vindictive, aggressive, or anything like that. The attack of the man would evoke pity.

This is where the scale ends. The man at the bus shelter can be progressively replaced by people of increasing relationship to us. We can all build our own individual scale. Above the bum is someone to whom we are indifferent or who is completely unknown to us, then comes perhaps a neighbor, followed by friends and workmates. Close friends and family members are even higher on the scale. The top rung is occupied by the person most important to us. This might be a parent, spouse, or child, or someone else whom we really love and respect, but most importantly, someone from whom we expect love and understanding.

The story can now be repeated, only this time, imagine that it is not a bum, but that most important person, who is treating you really badly. This can really get people down and cause pain, sadness, and even depression. Some respond aggressively and start arguing, fighting for better treatment. Others simply ignore it or remain silent. However, they become embittered and close their hearts and think, "You can't expect love or friendship in this world." To spontaneously respond sympathetically to the wrong inflicted by that most important person, by trying to see his frailty and immaturity without feeling superior ("They know not what they do[50]") is to be on the top rung of our scale. Compassionate love is the highest degree of independence.

THE FIVE LEVELS OF EMOTIONAL INDEPENDENCE
1. DEPENDENCE.
2. SYMMETRICAL CONFLICT.
3. AGGRESSIVE IGNORANCE.
4. ASSERTIVENESS.
5. COMPASSIONATE LOVE.

We see that we can be independent towards certain people, but not others. I might be able to embrace the shouting bum, but when someone close treats me badly, I become sad or behave aggressively. Examining ourselves to find our position on the scale is a worthwhile endeavour.

"A PERSON CAN FEEL MANY THINGS,
BUT THAT DOESN'T MATTER.
WHAT DOES MATTER IS THE ATTITUDE
OF THE WILL."

While our feelings perform an extraordinarily important function in our lives, we should not identify with them. It is important to understand that the SELF is not a feeling. The SELFcan feel this or

---

[50.] Lk. 23:34

that, but it is not defined by what it feels. "A person can feel many things, but that does not matter. What matters is the attitude of the will," according to Karol Wojtyła in the book cited above.[51]

Personal development involves gradually separating the SELF from our feelings. This separation does not consist in suppressing our feelings, but in a specific internal attitude that enables a feeling to be observed, and provides for a consideration of what it says about my inner self (not about what is happening outside me). A mature person feels a lot of things, but allows herself time to think about which decision to make. She will sometimes act in keeping with the promptings of her feelings, and sometimes in direct opposition to them. She sometimes remains passive and does nothing. This **separating ourselves from our feelings can be defined as living "in choice," as opposed to living "in feelings."**

"When I was a child, I used to talk as a child, think as a child, reason as a child; when I became a man, I put aside childish things," wrote St. Paul in his Hymn of Love.[52] Putting aside childish things means separating oneself from one's feelings. Not to do so is to remain "like a child," that is, infantile.

Take the feeling of hunger as an example. A newborn does not generally separate *himself from his feelings. When he feels hunger, all of him becomes hunger in a sense. That is why he cries. What he feels is all embracing. As the child grows (assuming he has wise parents), his decisions are made by his volitional center, which distances itself from his emotional center, so that while a hungry two-year-old will quickly have to be given something to eat, he will no longer cry. An older child can (and should) be taught to go hungry longer, and, in defiance of media advertisements, not satisfy hunger immediately. This child should be told "Wait. Lunch will be*

---

[51] Wanda Półtawska, op. cit. p. 48.

[52] 1 Cor. 13:11.

ready in an hour." This is not just a question of our convenience, it is an activity that helps the young person mature and learn that he can feel something unpleasant without having to respond immediately. In this way, the "I" so far distances itself from the "I FEEL" that someone on the verge of starvation becomes able give his last piece of bread to someone in need, if impelled to do so out of love.

The heroism of love would not be possible unless our feelings were separated from the SELF. That is why St. Paul mentions it in the Hymn of Love. An immature person who feels something unpleasant has to react immediately and reduce the discomfort. Moreover, it would be hard not to conclude that our society mostly consists of people who make feelings absolute and whose life's purpose is the pursuit of pleasant feelings. We also have problems with this during therapy, which frequently involves delving into unpleasant things.

Self-development in the domain of feelings appears to be a fundamental issue in therapy and human growth. We teach our clients to observe their feelings and detach themselves from them. We can often show them, through specific work with the body, how what they feel now refers back to their childhood and actually has very little connection with the present.

> WE SHOULD NOT WORK **ON** OUR FEELINGS (SO AS TO FEEL OR NOT FEEL SOMETHING), BUT **WITH** THEM (IN ORDER TO DISCOVER WHAT THEY HAVE TO CONVEY TO US).

Working with our feelings can be divided into direct work, which is undertaken when the feeling arises (especially when it is intense) and actual work, which is to be undertaken when the feeling subsides or completely disappears.

WORKING WITH FEELINGS:
1. DIRECT
(WHEN THE FEELING APPEARS).
2. ACTUAL
   (WHEN THE FEELING SUBSIDES OR
   COMPLETELY DISAPPEARS).

1.   DIRECT WORK WITH FEELINGS

Direct work consists in stopping while the feeling is still really strong. We encourage the adoption of an attitude that we call "**active silence.**" The first step is to "**not act**" and the second is to "**not speak.**" These two steps are equally important.

Nobody should need convincing that people who act on their feelings encounter a lot of misfortunes as a result. If we are waging war, and see that a powerful enemy is coming towards us, and we are not prepared for battle, then it would be irrational to take the enemy on. Retreating to the forest would be the wisest course of action in this situation. While this will not win the battle, we will still have a chance at winning the war. For this reason, the starting point for working with feelings is to develop the "stop" reaction when something triggers a powerful emotion in us.

Silence is the second major characteristic of the proper response to an intense feeling. This gives us the opportunity to look deeper and see more. The impulse to comment should be repressed. Some, under the sway of strong feelings, have a powerful need to share what they are feeling with others. They quickly try to find a solution. We encourage them to desist and remain silent. We suggest that they **write down what they are feeling (i.e. name the feeling),** the context in which the feeling appears, and the consequences of succumbing to it. It is worth waiting at least a day and observing the changes that have occurred in our emotional state during that time. It is really important to work with a sheet of paper. Letting the SELF write down what it felt almost lets us physically detach ourselves from what we are feeling. This places the feelings outside ourselves – on the sheet of paper.

The next phase of direct work is to **express what we feel**. Caution: This is not to be randomly blurted to just anyone. This is not about unburdening ourselves to our friends over a coffee or a beer. Working on our inner self consists in expressing what we are feeling to an emotionally integrated person, one who can view our problem(s) objectively and neutrally, and who will not hesitate to tell us difficult things if it is for our own good. That is because we are not concerned with consolation here, but in understanding what is happening inside us. This can be assigned to an empathetic person whom we trust. Difficult feelings are placed further away from us when they are expressed. In interviews, we mainly focus on what a given feeling tells us about ourselves, and not on the circumstances that evoke it.

Only afterwards can we ask about possible **actions or decisions**, always in the context of personal development, that is, in an appeal to Love with a capital "L." No action is to be taken until we get a clear answer.

DIRECT **WORK** WITH FEELINGS (ACTIVE SILENCE):
1. DO NOT ACT.
2. DO NOT SPEAK.
3. WRITE (NAME).
4. EXPRESS.
5. ACT?

---

2. ACTUAL WORK WITH FEELINGS

It often happens that an action to which we are then called is not directly connected with the situation that evoked the powerful feeling in us. The impulse to make a resolution and/or a change in life presents itself. This is what we mean by actual work. It takes place in the context of whatever it is that evokes the feelings in us, and not directly towards people and/or events to which we react emotionally.

This has a kind of desensitization all its own. When we are exposed to an allergen over a long period, our immune system loses its ferocious response. Likewise, we learn to observe the appearance, duration and cessation of our feelings. This is enormously important, especially in the case of difficult feelings, such as hunger, sadness, anger, exasperation, excitement, and so forth. Prayer, especially contemplation, plays an enormous role in working with feelings, as does a humane sense of humor that should allow the "ass of our emotional nature" to be expressed with warmth and wholeheartedness.

> ACTUAL WORK WITH FEELINGS TAKES
> PLACE IN THE CONTEXT OF WHATEVER
> IT IS THAT EVOKES THE FEELINGS IN US,
> AND NOT DIRECTLY TOWARDS PEOPLE
> AND/OR EVENTS TO WHICH WE REACT
> EMOTIONALLY.
> IT IS CONNECTED WITH THE SHATTERING
> OF THE FALSE SELF, AND INVOLVES
> A CONSCIOUS AND CONTROLLED
> ENTRY INTO THE SITUATIONS THAT
> EVOKE THE DIFFICULT FEELINGS.

III.

RELATIONSHIP WITH PARENTS

We sometimes think of living in simplicity and obscurity like the Holy Family when we speak of the spirituality of Jesus the Nazarene. However, Nazareth can also be thought of in terms of the difficulties that Jesus faced in his home town. The Savior had issues with Nazareth. The gospels recount that he could not perform any miracles there,[53] and that his family and close friends had suspicions that he was mentally ill.[54] The tension came to a head during an oration that Jesus gave in a synagogue. He began to refer to himself as the Messiah while berating his listeners for their closed hearts and minds. Infuriated, they seized Him and wanted to throw Him off a hill.[55] The townspeople of Jesus did not submit to the Good News. Nazareth stood in opposition to it.

We can all experience similar difficulties with our families and close childhood friends. Many adults experience startling "Nazarene feelings." These feelings can lead a manager of a large company, well versed in making difficult strategic decisions and managing a large group of people, to curl up in fetal position and cry out for his Mommy. Another person will go numb in the playground of her old elementary school. It often happens that families are reluctant to accept the changes in our lives or they

---

[53] Cf. Mark 6:5.

[54] Cf. Mark 3:21.

[55] Cf. Luke 4:16–30.

object to our life choices. They are sometimes the last to get the message that we have changed.

We are seldom aware that the current emotional attitudes and responses we have accepted are associated with our childhood, with what we call our "inner Nazareth," which is still opposed to the Savior and His new life.

> OUR "NAZARENE FEELINGS" HAVE THEIR ORIGIN IN OUR RELATIONS WITH OUR PARENTS, OUR SIBLINGS, AND OUR PEERS FROM OUR EARLY SCHOOL YEARS, AND THEY APPEAR IN VARIOUS SITUATIONS IN OUR ADULT LIVES THAT RESONATE WITH OUR PAST.

One woman says that she reacts aggressively to older men who remind her of her father, who walked out when she was a small child. Another person, who had a perfectionist mother, works without pausing for breath and cannot stop to rest for even a moment. Someone else sinks into an irrepressible melancholy when subjected to mild criticism. Examples like these are endless.

"Nazarene emotions" take us out of balance and into pain and isolation in their desire to "hurl us into the abyss." Many of us, although technically adults, still haven't left Nazareth. We have interminable debates with our parents – sometimes even deceased parents. We need to be aware of this and ask ourselves what our relations with our parents are right now, regardless of whether they are still living, when approaching personal development and working on ourselves.

If you want to determine whether you have already left your Nazareth, stop in that place for a moment and think of your parents (each individually) and describe what you feel towards them. If you are still resentful, hold any grudges, or feel any rejection, any kind of internal struggle or a complete lack of feeling, then your departure has not yet been accomplished internally. Anyone who has "left Nazareth" can look at his parents with equanimity. As an adult, he no longer expects anything from them or rejects anything about them. He is not out to prove anything and is not fighting over anything. He is not running away from them and is not dependent on them. That which is felt for them from the heart can be described as understanding and sincere kindness. He appears to be looking at his mother and father from the standpoint of eternity, as if they were all before the Lord. There is an inner reconciliation and an understanding that his parents were a link in the chain through which life has come. He can look at them like brothers and sisters. He is neither better nor worse than they are. We are their equals before God in the order of creation. No more claims. No more grievances. Just understanding and reconciliation.

This perspective brings profound peace and solace, and is a sign that leaving our parents has now been accomplished internally.

These "Nazarene feelings" have to be resolved. We have to leave our parents and our childhood behind before we can be integrated internally. Many people, even though they are starting to go gray, cannot manage this, as they have fallen into an enemy trap. Here we describe the major traps.

TRAPS THAT PREVENT US FROM LETTING
GO OF OUR PARENTS:

1. THE BLIND TRAP (DENYING OR NOT UNDERSTANDING OUR PARENTS' MISTAKES).
2. THE REGRET AND ETERNAL EXPECTATIONS TRAP.
3. THE DISOWNING OUR PARENTS TRAP.

1.   THE BLIND TRAP (DENYING OR NOT UNDERSTANDING OUR PARENTS' MISTAKES)

This is a peculiar blindness. This occurs when **someone fails to understand what went on in parental relationships and cannot see the facts as they actually were**. We tend to idealize our childhood because noticing our parents' mistakes evokes feelings of guilt. Having the conscious mind of an adult child admit the inconvenient facts, manipulations, and abuses perpetrated by her parents would peel away many layers of anger.

How is it that many people cannot see their parental relations for what they were in reality? Firstly, because **a child will harbour a perfect image of its parents for as long as it can**. A parent is everything to a child and so it does not want to see or comprehend what happened and which is sometimes still happening. Another reason might be that the child has been brought up to be loyal. The parent might have inculcated an ideal picture of him or herself from a very early age and not tolerated any dissent. He or she sometimes makes use of religion by twisting the biblical injunction to "Honor your father and your mother" to mean "Do not criticize or contradict your parents." This may give the child an idealized picture of both parents, although it more often leads to a polarization where one parent is completely bad and the other completely good: he was cheated on, or she was the one who brought me up and was close to me. It is worth paying special attention to the positive picture of the "better" parent, as idealization goes to the very essence of the trap we are talking about.

One man with anxiety neurosis told us that he had had a marvellous childhood, *full of wonderful memories, and that he had really good, caring parents. However, when we began to question him on the details, we learned that between the ages of one and four he was raised by his grandparents and saw his parents once a month, if that. This was because his parents ran a business and did not have time to look after him. His grandparents eagerly "adopted" him. When we told our client that we could think of better parents than ones that had abandoned their child for a couple of years, he sat there without saying anything for a quite a while, trying to digest our observation. And when we said that his grandparents had unwittingly wronged him by accepting him into their home (mature grandparents would have sent him back to his parents with the message: "He's our grandchild, but your child, and you have to take him") and that they might have been using him to alleviate their loneliness in their old age (while it all appeared to be so high-minded) he almost fell into a stupor. Bottling up his anger towards his parents and grandparents was the cause of his neurosis. The anxiety gradually began to subside once he stopped allowing this.*

Another case that comes to mind is that of a woman who came to us because she was prone to uncontrollable bouts of rage towards her husband and daughter. When we started to get down to childhood issues, it turned out that she had a wonderful, loving father and a cold and unfriendly mother. "Dad liked to play with me, but Mom got really angry." At first blush, it would seem that the mother was exploding with rage at her husband out of simple jealousy. However, after conversing further, it turned out that her dad only played with her after he had quarrelled with his wife, and only did so to make his wife angry. He was using the child, not playing with her. Her anger towards her father was repressed and every so often appeared in her family relations.

Falling into the "blind trap" happens fairly often because there is a lot of disorder in family relations.

For example, a father might have problems in his relationship with his son, who became the mother's main object of affection as soon as he was born (especially if he is the firstborn; this also affects daughters, although not as often). Women all but fall in love with the boy – while all but abandoning their husbands.[56] The father turns cold towards the son. He never praises him, as he sees him as a rival. He becomes aggressive towards his own child in his fight to maintain his place in the family. Obviously, he then becomes "the bad guy." However, the woman, who comes across as the "good guy" is the one who quietly engineered this entire sorry scenario and reinforces the whole negative setup by protecting the child from his father. The more she protects the child from his "bad father," the more aggressive the father becomes. The child is aware of his anger at his father, but not of his anger towards his mother. After all, she has always stood up for him.

The classic case is that of a child from a family in which one of the parents was an alcoholic or left for another relationship. It is easy to succumb to the illusion that it was that parent who had the problem and who bore full responsibility for the entire situation, while the other was merely a victim. The child cannot look into what happened before the infidelity or the compulsive drinking. There is no conception of those prior events, only the memory of awful childhood facts. The child does not understand that both spouses are most often responsible for the breakdown of a marital relationship. He often passes judgment, pronouncing "guilty" or

---

[56] It is exceptionally toxic whenever a child, seemingly infused with love, becomes the most important member of the family, or more important than either of the parents. This is discussed further in our book *Rodzice w akcji* [Parents in Action], Edycja Św. Pawła, Kraków, 2011.

"not guilty," unaware that this verdict is a gross, and often unjust, simplification.

We recall a man whose mother had a severe deprivation neurosis. The chief symptom was a pathological jealousy of his father (her husband). She threw tantrums over literally everything, which led to Dantesque scenes being played out at home. His father could not even look at another woman. The man decided to leave home while she was chopping wood with an ax in a frenzy. The son, who had been subject to his mother's hateful indoctrination since he was a small boy, had all avenues of contact with his father completely cut off. He assumed her hatred and never forgave his father for leaving home. He could not live an emotionally healthy life so long as he was caught in the "blind trap."

The "blind trap" is also set whenever a parent makes a child a confidante of her secrets and sufferings. This is especially common when a child is raised by a single parent or is drawn into an emotional alliance against the other parent in a marriage crisis where the spouses are fighting. This disorients the child. On the face of it, there is nothing wrong with either parent sharing her problems with the child. After all, isn't this a sign of confidence and love? Actually, no, it isn't. The parent who shares her cares with the child is burdening him.

The potent image of a parent holding her hands on the head of a seated child cropped up during group activities. The group was asked to comment. Someone said that he saw a blessing or a prayer of intercession. Someone else exclaimed "Not necessarily! The parent is leaning on the child and holding its head down, so that she cannot draw in the air for herself." Fear and recognition wafted through the group. A child does not know that what she understood to be support ("Mom was my best friend") was actually harmful ("and often told me about her issues with my father"). The person closest to her saved herself at the cost of her own child.

A similar mechanism comes into play when we deal with overprotective parents. There does not seem to be anything wrong with excessive care. More care means more love. However, **overprotection is aggressive by its very nature. It does not stem from love for the child, but from the guardian's anxiety for him or herself.** The child receives every gesture thinking "my Mom loves me." When, as an adult, he/she understands what was really going on, the tide of anger that has been held back for years suddenly bursts. The anger comes to save the child from its own parent. However, it is accompanied by an enormous feeling of guilt. How is it possible to be angry at a parent who has devoted her whole life to me? **A person can be imprisoned by unreleased Nazarene feelings.**

There are parents who "love" their children "for themselves" and "program" them for loyalty. They will not allow them to leave home, and keep them there on a leash of guilt. This is sometimes subtle, and sometimes blatant. The parents manage to "endow" a child with the gift of a home near their own residence, simply so that they can have a caretaker: "As you're the youngest, you can stay at home with us on the farm and look after us in our old age." Adult children find it hard to go their own way without feeling guilty. They cannot spread their wings because they feel they owe their parents something.

Children do not sign up for a debt towards their parents that has to be repaid over their entire lifetimes. Not everybody understands that the guilt they feel is not the response of a sensitive conscience, but a "Nazarene feeling" that has its source in improper family responses. It is worthwhile understanding this and making the decision to leave home, even despite this feeling, which will not immediately vanish as an emotional reaction. However, understanding enlightened by truth leads to freedom and helps resist pressure.

"Fair enough," someone will say, "but what about love for your parents in this situation? We, their children, are responsible for them in their old age, even legally." "Of course," we reply. This is not about getting us to cut off contact with our parents, and it is especially not about not caring for them when they are sick or elderly. **However, undertaking to care for our parents when they are in genuine need is one thing, but supporting them on their terms after we have left them physically, and especially emotionally, is something else entirely. And "care" that continues without letup from childhood, and which prevents the child from starting its own life, is something else again.** This has to be understood in order to live a productive life.

We call it the "blind trap" because **an adult who does not realize what was going on in his family home can find it difficult to leave Nazareth emotionally.** He can't manage to integrate even when his parents have been dead for years. Nazarene feelings demand truth and make their presence felt at unexpected moments, often leading to despair. Why is there so much anger inside me? Why am I anxious? Why do I feel guilty when I allow myself little pleasures? An adult who finds himself constantly in Nazareth will sometimes try to reform it, but **Nazareth has to be abandoned.** Even Jesus left so that he could productively carry out his mission.

A certain young woman never stopped worrying about her parents, especially her father, who was at the end of his tether, living with an alcoholic wife. The loving daughter sought help for her parents, who refused to make any changes that might have cured a sick situation. Their marriage crisis deepened: the mother drank more and more; the father steadily sank into depression; and our patient spent hours on the phone with him and her mother, and became increasingly worse herself. Both parents refused therapy, and the daughter was always ready to go to the family home when called out there in crisis situations. This went on for years.

She was completely taken aback when we told her that restricting her relations with her parents and starting to live her own life would be the best thing she could do for them. We told our patient that when her father phoned asking for help, she should respond calmly but firmly with, "No Dad, I'm not coming over. Call the police if Mom is drunk and making a scene. I'm busy. I love you both, but this is none of my business. You're adults and I've given you a phone number for therapy."

She needed time to understand that by helping the way she had, she had been unwittingly worsening the problem. Leaving to go your own way is the best thing you can do for your Nazareth.[57]

We now describe two remaining traps that prevent us from emotionally leaving our childhood behind. These lie in wait for anyone aware of the wrongs and injustices inflicted by their parents or peers.

2.   THE "REGRET AND ETERNAL EXPECTATIONS" TRAP

The second trap involves a child not leaving his parents emotionally, and sometimes not even physically, and constantly complaining, "Why didn't they give me any love? Why was it so awful? Love me. Love me!" **Expectations of love and acceptance that cannot be satisfied are unconsciously carried over to other relationships in life. The adult child continues to expect an environment of emotional gratification.** If married, this hunger for love is transferred to the spouse; if a parent, the expectations are transferred to a son or daughter. A need for love that was not satisfied in childhood has repercussions for a distinctive way of functioning. A person afflicted with an emotional yearning hangs around her parents or people who symbolize them, like someone leaning over an empty well. She would rather complain about the

---

[57]."But he [Jesus] passed through the midst of them and went away." (Luke 4:30).

lack of water in the well of her childhood than follow her own path and find her own well.

People who have fallen into this trap are typically extremely averse to self-development and finding the external causes of the problem, believing instead that others are at fault. Having failed to find emotional independence, or sovereignty, they build up expectations towards their surroundings, and finally start to resemble a black hole: they can never draw in enough. Instead of making a start on personal growth and self-development, digging their own well, they adopt a demanding attitude. They are sad and dejected, convinced that they are worthless, and that the world is wrong and people are mean. They feel misunderstood by those around them and are prone to weepiness. This, however, covers up a fierce rage that is manifested in bouts of aggression. The inner scream that continually breaks out of those who have fallen into this kind of trap is saying Love me! Notice me! Show me some interest!

The people around them initially try to meet these expectations. A husband in this trap will constantly show his affection, send texts every few hours, even when he is at work. His wife, pressured by his expectations, will try to surprise him. The community will try to console him and show him concern or interest. A friend will visit and say something nice. However, it will not be long before the return texts are too few and far between, the surprises are not what they should have been, the consolation is too shallow, and the visits too infrequent. "It's not enough!" is either stated outright or insinuated by an often histrionic characteristic attitude and behavior.

The way a person who is caught in this regret and eternal expectations trap functions is aptly described as "sucking blood without puncturing the skin." After a period of making strenuous efforts to show affection without seeing any improvement in the situation, **those around the person become worn out**. No mature person wants to tiptoe around emotionally starved people for long.

Guilt is the initial sentiment: "Maybe, we don't love her enough? Maybe we need to try harder? Anyone can see that there is not enough love in us...." Someone, however, will eventually notice the manipulation, lose patience, and become angry. **This most often results in the relationship being severed** and the "poor unloved child" is once more convinced that the world is wrong, nobody understands him and people cannot be trusted. **The emotional deficit deepens**, leading to a neurotic vicious circle that drives itself. The adult child will remain dissatisfied so long as he refuses to admit to this typical functioning to himself and does not take responsibility for his own life.

It often happens that an adult child of an alcoholic (ACA) comes to us for consultation. Typically, he actually announces this label almost from the outset. When asked why he has come, the response is "I'm an ACA." It can take quite a while to explain to someone like this that defining oneself as an ACA precludes any further therapy or development. What can be done with the fact that someone is an ACA? After all, he is an adult and the child of an alcoholic. We then like to provoke him a little. "If you're an ACA, there's nothing left for us to do but put a plaque on your tombstone with the inscription "Here lies an ACA. In honor of his memory..."

We obviously understand and respect ACA therapy, but it is not good for someone to finish therapy believing that he is an ACA. With this description, you can rationalize almost anything and dispense with the need for self-development. "Recognize the mechanisms of your FALSE SELF and stop describing yourself as an ACA. Don't define yourself this way, because it was your parents who drank. You are an ACG – an adult child of God! You still have a chance to change and grow. You don't have to be an ACA for the rest of your life. Your parents' alcoholism does not have to become your name!

It is worth adding, regarding those who fall into this second trap, that the depth of the emotional deficit does not depend entirely on what they objectively experienced in childhood. We sometimes meet people who have had really horrible childhoods, yet function better than expected as adults, considering what they have been through. Others, by contrast, come from families where it was "not all that bad," yet Nazarene emotions dominate the way they function. The depth of hurt therefore seems to depend not only on objective experience, but on childhood sensitivity as well. It may additionally be connected with adverse circumstances, such as the death of a close friend or relative, difficulty surrounding siblings, poverty, chronic illness in the family, and so forth.

3.   THE "DISOWNING OUR PARENTS" TRAP

This third trap is possibly the most insidious one, as **it gives the illusion of self-reliance**. To return to our image of the well, what we see here is a child who despises what little water there is to be had, and dies of thirst before he can dig out his own spring. The child rejects his parents and leaves with a feeling of self-reliance. This feeling, however, is an illusion.

In contrast to those constantly crying out for attention, these people typically spurn affection. They function emotionally as if they wanted to shout at their (sometimes deceased) parents: "See? I can manage perfectly well on my own! I don't need your or anyone else's help or support." They exhibit a lot of initiative and energy, stress self-sufficiency and resourcefulness, and are often successful in their professional lives. However, they either do not consider themselves worth all that much, or on the contrary, they take themselves too seriously and are extraordinarily narcissistic. They find it difficult to form relationships, as the prospect of entering into a long-term relationship induces a lot of anxiety. While those caught in the previous trap cling to others, these shun those close to them, and their hunger for affection intensifies. It would be humiliating for them to admit to this hunger.

Paradoxically, **this defensive attitude can bind people to their parents very strongly**. Those who fall into the independence trap most often replicate those attributes and mistakes of the rejected parent that they hate most. People who hate their mother or father unconsciously carry that parent inside them - sometimes for life.

> THE MORE WE REJECT A PARENT, THE MORE SIMILAR AND CLOSELY BONDED WE ARE TO THAT PARENT.

A typical example from our office is that of a businesswoman who graduated from two higher educational institutions. She is currently a company CEO. She is a perfectionist at work and is very well dressed and groomed. She is extremely demanding of herself and others. She has a wide circle of friends and is the life of any party. She leads a prayer group after hours. On the surface, she is someone to envy, piling success upon success. However, she comes to us for assistance with unidentified somatic symptoms. She also feels down. Extended discussions have revealed several problems. She is terrified of growing old. She is still single, and has not managed to enter into any relationships. She has taken up drinking in the evenings, and over time, has come to drink stronger liquor and more frequently. When asked about her relationship with her parents, she replied: "I'm in contact with my mother. I visit her occasionally. I don't even remember my father. He died a couple of years ago and I never visit his grave. He drank and he beat us. I want to forget him as quickly as possible." Until she opens up to what her father gave her (even if very little, or "only" her life) she will follow the same path as he did, and will never get close to another person. The woman needs to understand that what she regards as her achievements (financial, professional and emotional independence) is her defense mechanism and a trap that she will have to relinquish if she wants to grow. She has to learn how to relax, and she will find inactivity a challenge. She has to learn to overcome her anxiety and open herself up to relationships where she will lose her independence (but not her freedom). This road will take her through a discovery of her own vulnerability in the presence of others.

Both those who always expect love and affection, and those who reject their parents fall into the trap of emotional dependence. Some never leave the well because there is never enough water, others angrily dig into it and get nothing. They all need to be open to a solution that can be summed up in just one sentence:

> TAKE WHAT WAS GOOD
> AND GO YOUR OWN WAY.

There is always something to draw, even if there was not enough water. You must have received something, even in the darkest childhood. After all, you are alive and reading this text. Someone fed and clothed you. And even if your parents placed you for adoption immediately after you were born, you still got something from them – your life.

Take what is good and go your own way! But you will have to refrain from judging your parents first.[58] Our patients participate in various kinds of healing prayers to forgive their parents. These are obviously beneficial and justifiable in themselves. You can pray to forgive your father or mother, but you have to be careful to see that these prayers are not uttered from the standpoint of a child issuing the verdict: "My parents are culpable and I am magnanimously forgiving them." Obviously if some wrong has been inflicted (such as beatings, molestation, rejection, or negligence), there is something to forgive in the moral order. **But a child should not be**

[58.] Judging a person's actions is not the same as judging the person.

involved in judging or accounting for a parent. She should simply accept what was good and leave.

When children start to judge their parents, they resemble people who hold a grudge against a color-blind person for not painting or who rebuke a deaf person for not composing symphonies. Someone without arms could not have wrapped them around us.

OUR PARENTS GAVE US WHAT THEY HAD.
IT IS NOT FOR THEIR CHILDREN TO JUDGE WHETHER THEY COULD HAVE GIVEN MORE.

They functioned as best they could manage. There is no point complaining and there is no longer anything to expect. Parents cannot be scorned or rejected. **You simply have to lean over them with a gesture of farewell, and go your own way, grateful for your life.**[59]

We are only free to leave when we have waived all claims. Once the child relinquishes all claims, lets go of all regrets, and receives what is there to be received, even if only biological life, she starts to mature, leaves Nazareth, and becomes emotionally autonomous. There comes a point when she can look at her parents with understanding: "My father. My mother. It was good, but it was hard. It was beautiful, but it was horrible."

---

[59] The word "farewell" is used figuratively, to convey emotional harmony, and not to convey an actual farewell with drastically restricted contact, although this is sometimes (albeit fairly seldom) essential in the case of parents who have hurt their children especially badly. Additionally, we do not deem it necessary to have accounts-settling discussions with parents, where explanations are requested, or what we understood or what hurt us, etc., is shared.

IV.

NEUROTIC PAIN AND GROWING PAIN

It is natural to not want to suffer. Suffering is avoided if possible. The word "suffering" is commonly associated with great physical or emotional pain. For our purposes in this book, we use the word with a somewhat different meaning. **We define suffering as any discomfort that evokes the entire range of difficult and unpleasant feelings.** We do not necessarily mean intense pain, but rather something unpleasant that we would normally want to avoid. For our purposes, we focus on two of the many and varied kinds of suffering in life: neurotic and developmental (or redemptive).

THE TWO KINDS OF EMOTIONAL SUFFERING (OR PAIN) OF SPECIAL RELEVANCE TO DEVELOPMENT:
1. NEUROTIC – INVOLUNTARY AND UNAVOIDABLE;
2. DEVELOPMENTAL/REDEMPTIVE – VOLUNTARY AND AVOIDABLE.

Neurotic suffering is associated with having been hurt, and arises involuntarily. It can be persistent and the causes can be elusive. However, **there is definitely a cause and it can most probably be traced back to childhood.** It can be felt subjectively as dissatisfaction with life, sadness, loneliness, lack of peace, anxiety, difficulty in forming relationships, withdrawal, lack of self-confidence, shyness, rejection, feeling isolated, and so on. This is the kind of suffering that induces people to come to us for therapeutic consultation, and that gets people to turn to God for help.

Developmental or redemptive suffering brings a completely different set of problems. **This kind of suffering can be removed by simply steering clear of certain situations**, avoiding certain people, and not engaging in certain activities. So long as we are afflicted with neurotic suffering, whether we like it or not, this second kind of suffering will be something we tend to put off as long as possible, like one with a toothache may avoid a visit to the dentist.

Taking painkillers and putting off going to the dentist will clearly not solve the dental problem. We simply need to accept the distress that goes with a visit to the dentist if we want to alleviate a toothache. Otherwise, it will only get worse. **Let's treat pain with pain!** Anyone who wants to alleviate neurotic suffering will have to accept developmental suffering. There is no other option. Staying within the confines of emotional comfort ("This situation is already hard; why should I add to it?") and not consciously taking on developmental pain, increases neurotic suffering. Those who understand the logic of surpassing themselves will begin to experience freedom from suffering.

> AVOIDING DEVELOPMENTAL SUFFERING (STAYING WITH N THE CONFINES OF EMOTIONAL COMFORT) INCREASES NEUROT C SUFFERING.

What we say here about development is also applicable to therapy. People come to us and assign us the task of changing them in such a way that they will be able to do something or other. They sometimes seem to expect us to perform miracles or magic tricks. They want to grow without effort and actually think that this is possible. They are disappointed when we break it to them that therapy proceeds in the reverse direction. **Efforts have to be made to face uncomfortable situations before there can be any change or growth: decision and action come first, then change and personal development, not vice versa.** *Obviously, the course of this work has to be suitably adjusted, and nobody can be required to accomplish it in an area where he cannot cope. If someone has been unable to enter an elevator for years due to claustrophobia, we're not going to recommend activities that require him to do so. That would be ludicrous, as that is precisely why he has come to us. It quickly turns out, however, that the phobia is only a cover for some other real avoidance or suppression. It is an expression of a conflict of which he is not even aware, in a completely different area. And that is precisely where we get the patient to go.*

For example, this patient with claustrophobia might be surprised to discover that although he never experiences any anxiety in relation to his wife, he avoids the word "sorry" at all costs, even when he can see that he is obviously at fault. But to actually say so would be tantamount to admitting weakness, error or failure – not just to his wife but to others as well. This is the moment where it is revealed: this struggle is not about an elevator! (Obviously, not everyone suffering from a phobia has difficulty in showing their weaknesses.)

Avoiding developmental suffering increases neurotic suffering. We can see discomfort being avoided or postponed in every one of our patients. *In our opinion, a therapist who promises a patient that she can experience real and lasting change without having to expose herself to suffering is merely selling short-term consolation. We do not have a magic wand to change people without their getting involved. Nor do we have a crystal ball that we can peer into to see the decisions our patients should be making. Life has been difficult since the first sin, and personal growth demands a mindful approach to suffering (understood as discomfort). This is not merely about bearing life's hardships, but putting an effort into self-development. Returning to emotional health is neither easy nor pleasant. There is no shortage of people only too happy to pay for a session with a therapist and experience change without any input on their part, but that is never going to happen. Obviously, we do not place this message in the ads for our practice, as the number of patients would drop precipitously!*

We come now to an important conclusion: **personal growth almost always occurs in greater or lesser emotional discomfort.** Avoiding suffering holds us in place. Anyone who wants to move forward needs to remember that personal growth is almost always accompanied by difficult emotions, and sometimes real pain.

A certain young boy was sent to us by his parents after they had caught him smoking marijuana. As can be imagined, the youngster was not interested in therapy and only came to the session for the sake of peace. The conversation therefore touched on general matters, the meaning and purpose of life, his plans, and so forth. We remember the shock we got when the boy smiled frankly and innocently admitted: "The purpose of my life? To make as much money as possible, so I can do as little as possible!" He didn't even try to pretend to be talking about anything more, as he did not see anything shameful in it. A lot of people seem to live like this youngster (including parents), although they would never admit it so openly. They follow the path of least resistance, not only in material matters, but in spiritual and psychological ones as well. Exertion and difficulties are not welcome.

And you, dear reader? If you had to make a few telephone calls, and one of them will likely be unpleasant, which one would you start with? A pleasant one? A neutral one? Or that most difficult one? Most people put off emotionally unpleasant situations for as long as they can. But not everyone. Some do the exact opposite – and they are the ones who grow.

Jesus, who is our Spiritual Master and our guide on the road to personal development, spoke about this with pinpoint precision:

"Then Jesus said to his disciples, 'Whoever wishes to come after me must deny himself, and take up his cross, and follow me.'"[60] This is not just about accepting suffering, which accompanies us through life whether we like it or not. **Jesus also spoke about taking up our cross** (suffering, discomfort) **which we can refuse**. And we have to consciously deny ourselves in order to do so. We should add that we are not advocating here with living in perpetual torment or a certain kind of emotional masochism. Nobody, least of all Jesus, wants to deprive us of the joy of life. On the contrary, Jesus wants to restore joy for us, and He leaves a hint - **in His Resurrection** - that a state of freedom and peacefulness, and of being united with the Father, **can only be entered by consciously choosing discomfort. Whoever loves his life loses it.**[61] **Unless a grain of wheat falls to the ground and dies, it remains just a grain of wheat.**[62]

One of Jesus' best known statements on personal growth is the one he uttered during a nighttime conversation with Nicodemus: "You must be born from above."[63] These words are easy enough to read, but once we spend a few moments reflecting on their meaning in greater depth, we find that they presage suffering. Childbirth was an extraordinary adventure for the baby who is now resting peacefully in his mother's arms. Imagine if he went back in time, into that experience. His familiar, warm and safe world suddenly begins to shrink. Everything comes to an end. The umbilical cord briefly tightens in the birth canal. The baby is still not breathing with its own lungs but is not yet being given oxygen. It is suffocating and feels that it is dying. Jesus likens the path of Christian growth to childbirth because there are difficult emotions

---

[60] Matt 16:24.

[61] Jn. 12:25

[62] Jn. 12:24

[63] Cf. John 3:1-7.

along the way: fear, sadness, loneliness, pain, regret, and sometimes anger and refusal. People will sometimes say "I feel that my whole life is slipping through my fingers." They feel pain precisely because they are in the process of being born. It would be madness, however, to cram the baby back into the mother's womb. The path of personal development is one way. But how few consciously choose that path! **Those who do not step back, but endure unpleasant feelings, attain more profound change and liberation.**

The agreement between spirituality and psychology is astounding. Jesus does not promise his disciples things will be easy. **The road passes through the choice of suffering, but that is not the same as endless suffering.** The further we progress along this path, the more frequently we encounter joy, serenity, and good humor. We have inner harmony, we live spontaneously, without constant self-scrutiny, assertively expressing ourselves, without pretending or constantly adapting to the expectations of those around us. Inner freedom lets us be guided by genuine love. We are increasingly willing to make efforts because we can see that our efforts are worthwhile. We begin to see that what we initially considered to be nearly our death actually turned out to be our road to liberation. What awaits us is stunning. Our "womb," to which we were so attached, is a preparation for the life that awaits us. After a certain point, we not only cease to fear the next spasms, but start to look forward to them; we work with them in our desire to bring on this birth quicker.

Avoiding or putting off developmental suffering is the main reason people live in neurotic pain, on the fringes of their personalities, cut off from their own values, and in a state of peculiar unconsciousness and blindness. So let's not put off dying until the day of our physical death. We can be released earlier – in this life!

V.

WORKING WITH THOUGHTS

When we start to look more carefully into what is going on inside our thoughts, we can only confirm with astonishment how true Fr. Józef Tischner's facetious saying is: "It's as if someone in my head is doing my thinking for me." Thoughts can waft through our minds, and without realizing it we can come to firmly believe they are truth and they define us. However, we will not move forward unless and until we start getting our thinking straight. Quite a few people try to adjust their emotions, not knowing that it is our thoughts, and not our feelings, that are subject to our will. We can choose what we think; therefore our thoughts should receive our attention.

> ATTEMPTING TO MODIFY OUR FEELINGS
> IS HARMFUL, BUT WE HAVE THE RIGHT,
> AND EVEN THE RESPONSIBILITY, TO
> WORK WITH OUR THOUGHTS.

It is absolutely essential to choose what we want to think and not simply agree with whatever goes through our minds.

As with life choices, thoughts can come from the REAL or the FALSE SELF. People sometimes discover to their horror that almost everything that they have ever thought about themselves, the world, and their relations with others comes from this other contaminated source. Beliefs about our own diminished or inflated worth, and beliefs about God, the world, and others can all be the handiwork of the FALSE SELF. How can we tell? It can be verified by examining the conformity of our own thoughts with universal truths and natural law. Christians know this as the Word of God. What would God be saying about me, others, and the world if He were thinking what I'm thinking? If our thoughts do not line up with divine revelation, then they are deemed to come from the FALSE SELF. Can they be "true thought" if they do line up?[64] **"True thought," in the psychological conceptualization, leads to love (that is, personal development). This stands in contrast to those thoughts dictated by the FALSE SELF, which hamper personal development and render love impossible.** In spiritual theology, thoughts emanating from the FALSE SELF are often identified as temptation.

The idea of working with thoughts is unacceptable to many schools of therapy, as it is considered an unwarranted intrusion into the patient's life. They hold that therapy should maintain a position of ideological neutrality, as "truth is relative and the patient constructs her own world," etc. We recognize this and we understand the assumptions underlying it.

Our conception, which we call Christian Integrated Therapy (CIT), recognizes the existence of objective truth: there is "up and down" in the world; good and evil exist; one way of thinking is healthy and true, and another is not; some attitudes towards life lead to greater love and inner freedom (that is, personal growth) while others hold us in place, and can even be harmful. According to CIT, the therapist should not hesitate to point out mistaken or misguided thinking, whether it be theological or psychological.

In our experience, the neurotic process is very often based on a mistaken understanding of love, human relations, freedom, and religion. Many people feel a significant improvement, or even a complete return to health, when they change their way of thinking. Although we are Christians, we also offer our therapy to non-

---

[64] Caution has to be exercised, however, as not everyone can correctly assess what does, and what does not, accord with the Word of God. People are often fed false theology.

believers, provided they are prepared to accept the assumption that there are certain universal truths in the world.[65]

We do not tell anyone how they should live ("You should change jobs"), what decisions they should make, or when they should make them ("It's high time you get married") during therapy. We cannot be responsible for someone else's life. Nor would we want to be. We are supposed to be guiding people towards maturity. However, we present developmental directions, the necessity for change, or the possible consequences of refusing change.

Someone we accompany might not able to identify true thoughts unaided and so we have to help, sometimes by directly demonstrating that what he has been accustomed to consider to be the truth is not the truth. We come now to the tricky terrain of recommending what to do. This is obviously related to fundamental truths about ourselves, and our relations with others and God. An accurate thought about feelings, prayer, love, and other areas that affect our emotional health sometimes has to be restored. Working in this sensitive area requires a lot of tact and patience. The patient can only entertain another thought when she understands the error in her former reasoning. This cannot be achieved by force, by the order of the therapist. **We do not change people by force; it simply is not possible. Rather, we accompany them in reaching understanding and recognizing truth.** *To demonstrate "true thinking" is not to create a person in our own image. We seek out*

---

[65] For example: *The worth of an individual does not depend on his skills, appearance, education, wealth, or intelligence. Human life is invaluable. Love should not be equated with feeling. Lying and betrayal are bad. Intentionally committed evil never leads to personal development. We are all of equal worth. Dividing feelings into positive and negative is mistaken and harmful. God, however understood, is love. There exists a higher power that guides every individual towards personal development. This development is oriented towards greater love, freedom, and emotional sovereignty. We denote certain attitudes and behaviors sins, because they are, by their very nature, harmful to both those who commit them and those who experience them. A sin is not a good forbidden by God, but an attempt to achieve a purpose in a way that is damaging to ourselves and others. A neurotic is someone who tries to fulfil a legitimate need for love in a self-destructive way. Neurotic behaviour is misdirected self-care. God's answer to sin is mercy, not punishment. Parents should not burden their children with their marital difficulties, etc.*

what is true with the person. We do not correct her political views, preferences, habits, etc.

Many people need an outsider, a mature person who has been down a certain road, with whom they can ascertain which thinking is mistaken and which is correct; which thoughts are the products of neuroses and are responsible for dysfunctions, and which have to be taken as true and deliberately chosen. **This involves deciding "what I choose to think" at the intellectual level, not "what I happen to be thinking."** We sometimes build a collection of true thoughts and beliefs from the bottom up with the client, which he then takes to be a sort of "constitution" against which all his views can be compared. It is then that the laborious work of self-development begins. This consists in rejecting what he does not choose to think, and what is still automatically imposing itself on him.

It is amazing how many people very grudgingly reject mistaken thinking, even when they concur, at the conscious level, that they have a mistaken view of reality.

One day, a woman who persistently considered herself inferior to others came to us. The mantra "I'm worthless, I look hopeless, I never get anything right," kept playing in her head. She obviously agreed that none of this was true, but only very begrudgingly decided to abandon these lies. There came a certain point when, almost backed up against the wall, she claimed, "I'll get nothing in return if I abandon them, I'll have to start working on myself, and I won't be able to hide behind these feelings..." The thoughts she expressed were actually a special defense mechanism, which magically absolved her of all responsibility for her own life. It was strange that she came to us for help, but at the same time, she resisted any change in her mindset. She wanted the "new" without dispensing with the "old."

We have to tell you in all seriousness that she was by no means exceptional in this. **Virtually everyone to whom we suggest making a clean break from false thinking resists at first.** *It is as if they regret* *losing something valuable, even if they intellectually agree that their thinking is erroneous and hampering their personal development.*

Thoughts emanating from the FALSE SELF can imitate true thoughts very convincingly.

We recall going to the mountains with some friends. A trip that should taken a few hours ended up taking almost twice as long and we were dead tired when we got there. At one point, one of our friends, who is a wonderful, intelligent, and magnanimous person, reached the end of her emotional tether. She completely lost it, which she later regretted. The next day, after we had rested, she told us: "You see, the truth about me has been revealed. You could see what I'm really like." We quickly contradicted her, because although she seemed to be discarding the sham to reveal the genuine, and while she might even have sounded apologetic, what she saying was coming from the FALSE SELF. "Has this trying event in the mountains made anything about all the love and devotion you put into your family not genuine? So what's the truth about you? A moment when your weakness revealed itself? Or the life that you lead every day and the attitudes that you consciously choose? Because, in reality, you want to love and you've succeeded admirably for most of your life. You're definitely capable of love and this can be seen every day. This episode showed that you react aggressively when you're physically exhausted. But aggression is not the truth about you."

To return once more to the advice of Karol Wojtyła: "I must tell myself clearly what I desire, and extract from what I desire those elements of which my will substantially approves."[66] This is a very important sentence. We are defined by what we choose, not by what we do. We should not be judged through the lens of our weaknesses, deficiencies, and shortcomings.

Imagine archaeologists unearthing an ancient vase, broken in pieces. Unfortunately some bits are missing, but because the vase

---

[66] Wanda Półtawska, *op. cit. p.* 48.

is so unique, beautiful, and priceless, it is cemented back together and placed in a museum, so that people can look at this wonderful find. Nobody comes to look at the gaps left by the missing fragments. They come to see what was recovered. So we too, while acknowledging our weaknesses, should not define ourselves by what hasn't worked out for us, but by what we want to make work.

If you were dealing with a man who was a wonderful husband and father, who lived very selflessly, and who did a lot of good, but who, despite many years of trying to fight it, still visits pornographic websites and masturbates, would you consider him an "unregenerate sinner"?

> WE ARE DEFINED BY THE GOOD
> THAT IS ALREADY WITHIN US,
> AND BY THE GOOD THAT WE DESIRE.
> GOOD ACTUALLY EXISTS, WHEREAS EVIL
> IS MERELY A LACK OF GOOD.
> WE ARE DEFINED BY WHAT EXISTS,
> NOT BY WHAT IN REALITY DOES NOT.

We obviously do not exhort people to ignore or shrug off their sins and weakness, but to be careful of what they think about themselves. A pilgrim can be both one who has already reached the place of pilgrimage and one who still has a very long road ahead.

> YOU HAVE TO AVOID PILING UP THE
> IMAGINATION.

In addition to the classic untrue thoughts that come from the FALSE SELF, we have to mention states of mind in which we do not stay in reality, but are diverted towards fantasy. **Our mind has** a tendency to run forward towards something that lies ahead, and to run backward towards something that has happened in the past. Either way, we are divorced from reality, because neither a dream, nor a fantasy, nor a memory is actually happening in the here and now.

What are rightly called planning and drawing conclusions have to be clearly distinguished from situations where our thoughts involuntarily put us in a world that does not really exist. Again, we quote our master, Karol Wojtyła: "**You have to avoid piling up the imagination**".[67] If you have ever spent hours debating in your head with someone who is not physically there, you will know what we're talking about. Some people manage to carry on internal fights like this for years. They argue with dead people and these virtual quarrels affect their mood. Others spend hours analyzing, "what would have happened if…" or "what will happen if…". Still others retreat into a dream world or indulge in fantasies, and believe me, they are most unhappy to hear that they should brutally expunge all these thoughts. "What am I supposed to think instead?" they ask. And that is a very good question.

A certain man told us his story as follows:

"A couple of years ago I was hurt by people who meant a lot to me, and seeing them aroused enormous resentment at the way I had been treated. My efforts to feel good and forget it came to nothing. Not only did anger, sadness, and regret well up inside me, but also interminable arguments that were supposed to prove that I was in the right, and that I had been treated most unfairly and badly hurt.

"My adversaries expressed neither remorse nor regret. On the contrary, they were perfectly convinced that they had behaved fairly towards me and had nothing to reproach themselves for. This

---

[67] Ibid.

provoked even greater internal disputes that resulted in such intense anger that it literally left me physically shaking whenever I saw those who, I believed, had hurt me. I felt bad about this and I was annoyed with myself because it seemed the way I thought and felt was far removed from loving my enemies. 'Since I couldn't stand the sight of those who, after all, weren't mortal enemies, how was I going to love real enemies?' I thought, and became really dejected.

*"And finally, a miracle occurred. During a liturgy, I was standing in church and torturing myself, when it suddenly hit me that I was being tempted. Pure and simple. I realized that the temptation was very subtle because it was happening in my head and I had the impression that 'I think the way I think,' and yet, at the very deepest level, I had chosen some other way of thinking! First, I decided to consider that my adversaries really did not understand that they had hurt me and so there was no point expecting them to be remorseful. Second, **I decided to choose to love them** and never speak ill of them to anyone, and when we met in other circumstances, I would want to smile and be kindly disposed towards them. **"It is my choice and only my choice that matters"** I declared inwardly. 'That being the case, I will treat any thought inconsistent with my choice as "alien," and as having trespassed on my mind, and I will firmly evict it from the premises. **I have chosen love and I must therefore not torture myself by not forgiving.** To this end I will take responsibility for what I choose, but not for what might be imposing itself on me against my will. Amen!'*

"It's hard to describe the relief I felt at that moment! It was as if I had been relieved of a heavy burden. I felt freedom and joy, and to my surprise, the thoughts that had until then been swirling inside me instantly dispersed. They were simply gone! My head only contained thoughts that I had chosen! Everything was cut off as with a sword by a single internal decision and a choice of will. The old thoughts made several more attempts to intrude on my territory over the following few months, but sporadically and with decidedly less confidence, and my 'internal response force' recognized them as alien. After six

months, they disappeared! And I felt that grace had prevailed in my life."

Our patient was unaware that the battle of thoughts being waged in his head was almost exactly what the Desert Fathers described.[68]

We can learn about working with thoughts from the Desert Fathers. The Fathers spent years putting their thoughts in order. Various maxims credited them with a great deal of determination in this area. A trace of this work can also be seen in the description of Jesus being tempted in the desert. It is typical of Jesus that after rejecting each of the devil's temptations with the Word of God, he inserted true thinking.[69] This tradition is hundreds of years older than modern psychological scholarship. The Fathers taught that the correct response to temptation was to substitute unsolicited and unwanted thoughts with short Biblical passages. Ardent and frequently repeated acts of prayer such as, "Jesus, I trust in You," "God is love," "God loves me as I am," and "I can do all things through Christ who strengthens me," are excellent for driving out thoughts emanating from the FALSE SELF.

People who have wrestled with their thoughts sometimes speak of having a subjective impression that the new, true way of thinking is artificial. The thoughts they are supposed to reject, they take to be natural, and those they acknowledge to be true, they take to be false and mismatched. This is perfectly natural. It is the result of having had false thoughts for many years, sometimes for as long as they have been aware. It takes about two years of self-development

---

[68] Evagrius Ponticus (345-399), a monk from Pontus and one of the most illustrious Desert Fathers, formulated a typology of eight passions that pervaded the human mind following original sin. The οκτώ λογισμοί (eight thoughts), according to Evagrius' typology, were the eight cardinal sins for which passionate thoughts that interfered with prayer and tempted people to sin were responsible.

[69] Cf. Luke 4:1–13.

to reverse this impression. Thoughts emanating from the FALSE SELF will then be instantaneously identified and rejected. We encourage patients to seize a false thought. The idea is to write out a sort of creed on a card and practice repeating it. This should contain true thoughts which the patient is to treat as her own "dogmatic constitution," repeat several times daily in her spare time, and learn by heart.

Clearing the mind of thoughts and beliefs emanating from the FALSE SELF is like ridding a city of uninvited and unwelcome visitors. At first it is difficult to distinguish "us" from "them." To ensure that the city only has lawful residents, everyone's identity will first have to be checked. The city guard then needs to staff the ramparts and check the identification of anyone who wants to enter the confines of the walls. The boundaries are gradually pushed out until, eventually, the guards are far away on the outer gates, saying: "Stop! Who goes there?" If the thought does not come from the REAL SELF, it will not be allowed to pass. Experience shows that this sort of change is eminently possible, and after a while the person working on her self-development will wonder how she could ever have thought the old way.

Thoughts should not graze like sheep without a shepherd. Nor should they wander wherever and whenever they want. Otherwise, one will get tangled in briars, or fall off a cliff, along with the shepherd. This cannot be allowed to happen. It is sometimes necessary to resort to various methods and tricks. If nothing helps and thoughts from the FALSE SELF are writhing around like snakes, then it would be better to turn on the radio, listen to an audio book, or call someone, so as to turn your mind to something else, doing whatever is humanly possible to block the voice of the FALSE SELF. Mindfulness techniques that focus attention and consciousness on "what is" can be a great help here.[70] And from there it is a small step to focus on The Only One Who IS. **Mindfulness in everyday activities, especially those that do not involve the intellect, is the first step towards permanent prayer**, in which we remain conscious of God the whole time. We have at our disposal, the wonderful Christian tradition of the Western and Eastern Church. Quite a few mindfulness techniques, based on the psychology of Buddhism, have appeared recently. While obviously these techniques are not prayers in themselves, they can help calm the mind.[71] However, before referring to them, we have to acknowledge and be confirmed in our own rich tradition.

Before closing this chapter on thoughts, let's spend a moment on the difference between what we call "working with thoughts" and what usually goes by the name of "positive thinking." We would like

---

[70] For example, when I fry cutlets, I fry cutlets. That is, I take care of my task, so that my mind stays focused on what I am doing right now, unless I am meditating on the Word of God during simple everyday activities.

[71] The Second Vatican Council Declaration on the Relation of the Church to Non-Christian Religions (para. 2) states inter alia: From ancient times down to the present, there is found among various peoples a certain perception of that hidden power which hovers over the course of things and over the events of human history; at times some indeed have come to the recognition of a Supreme Being, or even of a Father. [...] Thus in Hinduism, men contemplate the divine mystery and express it through an inexhaustible abundance of myths and through searching philosophical inquiry. They seek freedom from the anguish of our human condition either through ascetical practices or profound meditation or a flight to God with love and trust. Again, Buddhism, in its various forms, realizes the radical insufficiency of this changeable world; it teaches a way by which men, in a devout and confident spirit, may be able either to acquire the state of perfect liberation, or attain, by their own efforts or through higher help, supreme illumination. Likewise, other religions found everywhere try to counter the restlessness of the human heart, each in its own manner, by proposing "ways," comprising teachings, rules of life, and sacred rites. *The Catholic Church rejects nothing that is true and holy in these religions.* She regards with sincere reverence those ways of conduct and of life, those precepts and teachings which, though differing in many aspects from the ones she holds and sets forth, nonetheless often reflect a ray of that Truth which enlightens all men. [...] *The Church, therefore, exhorts her sons, that through dialogue and collaboration with the followers of other religions, carried out with prudence and love and in witness to the Christian faith and life, they recognize, promote and preserve the good things, spiritual and moral, as well as the socio-cultural values found among these men* (emphasis added).

The Decree on the Mission Activity of the Church (para. 18) states: [...] Let them reflect attentively on how Christian religious life might be able to assimilate the ascetic and contemplative traditions, whose seeds were sometimes planted by God in ancient cultures already prior to the preaching of the Gospel (emphasis added).

Therefore anyone who unequivocally identifies non-Christian Eastern religions with occultism, or even Satanism, is clearly at odds with the teaching of Vatican II.

to stress that the similarities are superficial, whereas the differences that result from practicing them are fundamental.

> THERE IS A FUNDAMENTAL DIFFERENCE BETWEEN POSITIVE THINKING
>
> AND TRUE THINKING.

Positive thinking is a vague concept. It is frequently understood as strengthening oneself through positive affirmations, and/or as creating one's own reality, and/or in believing that this way of thinking magically guarantees success, health, and prosperity.[72] While we are not always dealing with an occult version of positive thinking, this is often brought in to build a friendlier and more positive FALSE SELF. **Repeating formulas such as "I am strong," I can manage," "I can do it," "I will be successful," etc. to yourself is simply building castles in the sand**. It might feel a little nicer and more comfortable inside, but they have no foundation. **A self-affirmation does not deliver any health benefits. On the contrary, it is injurious to health, because it has no basis in fact.**

For example, the affirmation "I can manage," is just as false as the observation "I can't manage." A true thought would look something like: "I want to manage this and I'm going to do whatever I can to make it work. I hope I can do it, but it won't be the end of the world if I don't. My value as a person does not depend on it. If possible, I'll try again." It is plain to see that there is a fundamental difference between positive thinking and true thinking. **Obviously, a positive thought may happen to be a true thought, but it has to be stressed that this is not always the case.** This is why we have

---

[72]·A classic example are those books and films titled "The Secret of...". These are spiritually and psychologically harmful.

introduced the concept of "true thinking" in contradistinction to "positive thinking."

VI.

SMASHING THE "FALSE SELF"

There comes a point when working with grace requires drastic steps to smash the defense mechanisms that detach us from reality: from God, ourselves, and those close to us. We will call this smashing the FALSE SELF. This can be done passively or actively.

SMASHING THE FALSE SELF:
1. PASSIVELY.
2. ACTIVELY.

1.   PASSIVELY SMASHING THE "FALSE SELF"

Passively smashing the FALSE SELF involves embracing our own personal history. This means not merely acquiescing to whatever happens, but something significantly beyond that. We can choose to work with every reality – every event, situation, relation, internal and external state, in which we find ourselves, admitting no **exceptions.** This seems easy on the face of it, but an honest look into ourselves is enough to show myriad situations in which we experience inconsistency and discord within ourselves. Our thoughts and speech, which are full of bitterness, complaints, and even curses, usually give us away. And when these have been brought to heel, we are betrayed by our feelings, which show what our collaboration with our personal history really looks like. This is obviously not about seeing evil and injustice in the world or becoming an impassive stoic. It is about our internal attitude to difficult events.

We start to smash the FALSE SELF passively when we stop categorizing the events that life has brought us as either "good" or "evil." We are obviously entitled to consider them easy or difficult, pleasant or unpleasant.[73] However, we can survive even the most tragic situations in such a way that they will develop us internally and ultimately serve our personal growth. Unless we consciously decide to work with the hardships and pain that life brings, they will break us and make us bitter, regretful, contemptuous, and/or unforgiving.

From now on, I refuse to transfer responsibility for what happens to me onto external circumstances. Whatever comes may be grace. Anything can ennoble me – even (and perhaps especially) the most trying situations.

THINGS ARE TO US
AS WE EXPERIENCE THEM.

It is up to us whether experiencing difficult circumstances leads to growth and cleansing, or whether we begin to despair and feel sorry for ourselves. **The same difficult conditions lead to saintliness in one and separation from God in another.**

We once met two elderly habited nuns while visiting a cloistered convent. When we greeted them, one of them told us sadly that old age was no joy, at which the other became indignant and exclaimed with a smile: "It is a joy!" We were astounded that two people, who had spent almost their entire lives behind the walls of a convent, in

---

[73.]This is similar to how we view feelings.

the same conditions, and whose state of health was similar, could describe their situation in such diametrically opposite ways.

There comes a stage where it is not possible to develop further without a quiet acquiescence to grace: "Do with me what you will. Cleanse me of that which requires cleansing. I want to head quickly towards freedom." **What the will gravitates towards is important.** If my will is set on disarming the FALSE SELF, then at the deepest level of its choices, I will work with whatever comes, even if my initial impulse is to rebel or despair.

"Father, give me your Spirit, and I will gratefully accept every humiliation and adversity that comes to me." I (Marcin) composed this "risky" song as a prayer for collaborating with grace. We would like to disclose our own experience here. This prayer is always heard and heard very quickly. But it is not pleasant. (We won't put it any stronger than that). We pray that way every once in a while, but not too often, so that we can endure the apparent intense way this prayer is answered. If we wish, we can ask God to reveal the defense mechanisms that the FALSE SELF has hidden from us.

It is definitely worthwhile to examine how we respond to people, situations, and events we find difficult. Refusing to work with them is virtually tantamount to avoiding disarming our defense mechanisms. Obviously, this does not mean that we are not going to respond when someone is constantly hurting or humiliating us or when some moral evil is afoot, as we are learning humility right then and there. **We sometimes have to set boundaries, and we sometimes have to walk away and withdraw, because love requires us to do so. We should never abandon activities that could put an end to some evil.** It is not always easy, however, to tell whether we are doing something because we are genuinely seeking to do good or whether we are subtly shielding the FALSE SELF as well. And one does not exclude the other. This is one reason why we need an outsider to help us evaluate our real motivations for what we do.

2.   ACTIVELY SMASHING THE "FALSE SELF"

It is no mean feat to embrace to your own history, to see grace in everything, and meet the challenge of the Lord's Prayer – "Thy will be done" – with your heart. However, we can go even further. **We can intentionally enter into situations that are unbearable to the FALSE SELF. We can expose ourselves to contact with people we do not like, we can deliberately do things that make us feel very uncomfortable emotionally.** And this is really worth doing – not just not avoiding uncomfortable situations, but actually welcoming them.

> ONE OF THE MAJOR BASTIONS OF THE "FALSE SELF" IS OUR CONCERN FOR HOW THOSE AROUND US RECEIVE US.

Image anxiety makes many people to conform to other people's opinions. The fear of rejection is so strong that most of the time these people live based upon what others think. Everything is pre-filtered through the desire to perform and be put on display, or through the fear of being laughed at. Image anxiety is what causes some people to shut themselves off, others to constantly observe the reactions of those around them, yet others to control their emotions at all times, and again others to tell jokes incessantly. People behave as if their lives depended on being accepted by those around them. Their fear of embarrassment is so strong that it paralyzes their spontaneity, their decisions, and their actions.

We should not be indifferent to those close to us, but neither should our actions be determined by whether they accept what we do or what we are. Jesus often did things that did not please those around Him. We should boldly adopt positions that we find uncomfortable for our image. This does not mean acting provocatively, but simply being ourselves. Image anxiety is not overcome by reading interesting psychological books or by internal reflections. **You have to start by taking small steps in an uncomfortable direction – one that evokes embarrassment and/or tension; all the while asking God for the virtue of courage**. Bear in mind that courage does not replace anxiety; it exists alongside it. Courage does not put up with anxiety; it vanquishes it. It takes tremendous determination to break down the FALSE SELF. It won't go quietly. It will always put up a fight.

Once, when we were running a retreat with therapeutic activities, a woman asked us for a private interview. She complained of being bothered by a hand tic that was seriously hampering eating: "As soon as I sit down at the table with other people, the tic appears and causes a great deal of discomfort and embarrassment. I can't eat soup in peace because I spill it all over the table. It's really difficult for me. I've tried everything to get rid of this problem."

After some reflection, we asked her whether she really wanted to be rid of it, as we thought we had found a good way to move forward. She said that she wanted to, more than anything, and that she was prepared to do anything because she was so tired of it. "Well then," we said, "Let's start at the earliest opportunity by announcing this problem of yours before a meal." This suggestion nearly sent her into a panic. She protested vigorously. The woman's real problem was not her tic, but her embarrassment. Everyone at the retreat had their own specific personal difficulties (they would not have been at a retreat with therapeutic activities if they didn't), but they were almost all united in their embarrassment. We laughed and gently teased her: "But you were prepared to do anything." However, nothing would induce her to agree to our proposal. Her image anxiety was too strong. Even though nobody would have been surprised or shocked, and even though there is a mood of acceptance of human weakness on therapeutic retreats, she was completely frozen by the fear of being rejected.

We should add that after two days she conquered her FALSE SELF and publicly disclosed her problem (which, by the way, was evident to those around her). There were significantly fewer uncontrollable hand twitches almost immediately, and she good-humoredly laughed at herself at each meal. And so her therapy began. It was nice to watch her gain her freedom.

TALKING ABOUT YOUR WEAKNESSES,
GOOD HUMOR,
AND TRUTHFULNESS
ARE IMPORTANT STRATEGIES
FOR CRUSHING THE FALSE SELF.

We do not encourage exhibitionism or imprudently talking about intimate things. Certain matters should not be confessed publicly. However, it is really worth being determined to disclose your weaknesses, misfortunes, and failures. For some, it might be a huge problem to tell people in the office that it was hard to park. Another might have hidden her inability to swim from her friends for years. It might be the end of the world for someone else to briefly interrupt a conversation to ask the meaning of a difficult word. Others cannot bring themselves to say things like "I can't cope" or "I'm struggling." Still others pretend that they have read books or seen films that are being discussed at a party. Denial, projecting your weaknesses onto others, and camouflage are all FALSE SELF strategies aimed at building or defending an artificial image. The FALSE SELF loathes the words "Sorry," "I was wrong," and "I made a mistake."

Marcin: I remember how Monika and I once quarrelled just before setting off on a long-awaited weekend for just the two of us. We got into the car without a word and drove to our destination in silence. I felt that I should be the first to break the silence by saying I was sorry, but I almost fainted when I tried to utter these magic words. I observed myself and I could only marvel at the strength of my FALSE SELF. I felt that I'd die if it was me who made the first move towards reconciliation. I eventually decided that I'd count to ten and say it when I'd finished. So I counted one, two, three... slower and slower, but I persisted. When I got to ten, I said "sorry" like an automaton. Monika immediately said "I'm sorry too," and joy, love, and peace returned. We were saved once again.[74] **The gateway to humility is always open, but sometimes nobody wants to be the first to pass through it.** *The FALSE SELF cannot get through this gate.*

While most people go through all sorts of contortions to hide their weak points, some people's FALSE SELF announces the opposite position: "I'm no good, nothing ever works out for me in life," etc. They often sink into depression and irritability, and withdraw from social life. Grumbling is their preferred form of expression. Those who repudiate praise or appreciation of their work or appearance with "Oh that, it's nothing special..." belong to this group. This attitude has nothing to do with modesty or humility. It is yet another FALSE SELF disguise. These people should practice emphasizing their skills and their wins verbally. They need to learn to smile and joke, especially at themselves (they are habitually serious or sad), and to start conversations.

Joaquín Navarro-Valls, a spokesman for Pope John Paul II, once said in an interview that one of the things he learned from the Pope was to **"be in a good frame of mind, not through disposition, but by force of will."** This shows that we can put a smile on our face through an act of will, even when it is difficult. You can smile for the sake of others, so that they can feel that you love them. You might not be in the mood for jokes and only listen to them to dismantle the FALSE SELF, which generally hates good humor. Nothing is healthier than laughing at yourself.

---

[74] This story became the basis for "Secret Dialogue", which can be heard at the end of the track "Aybyśmy stali się jednością" [That we may become one] on the album *Milczę i kocham* [I'm quiet and I love].

While on the topic of the cheerful demeanor that we adopt, with some effort, despite ourselves, we should point out that there are also people who always joke in company, who constantly amuse those around them, and with whom it is hard to have a serious conversation. This cheerful superficiality is their defense mechanism, the game they play with those around them. Their path to self-development lies in keeping quiet and speaking seriously.

We should also take note of whether we are honest and truthful. Here, the principle that "everything we say shall be the truth, but not necessarily the whole truth" applies. We need to bear in mind that **truth, spoken at an inopportune moment or without love, can be very hurtful**. Not even Jesus spoke the whole truth.[75] However, Jesus is the Truth. For this reason, we need to take care that we are honest and sincere – no embroidering, glossing over, manipulating or evading to suit our own convenience. The FALSE SELF is behind every instance of not telling the truth. Testing yourself right now for sincerity, fairness, and honesty can be a very interesting exercise. Whenever we bend the truth, our defense mechanisms are plain to see. We cannot make light of even seemingly trivial fibs here.

One wise person told us how she learned to always tell the truth. She decided that whenever she caught herself out in even the tiniest lie, she would go back and rectify her little deception. This seems to be a very quick cure for telling little fibs.

> THE ROAD TO PERSONAL DEVELOPMENT
> DEMANDS DETERMINATION AND
> COURAGE.
> ONLY DECISIONS CAN CHANGE YOUR
> LIFE.

[75.]"I have much more to tell you, but you cannot bear it now. But when he comes, the Spirit of truth, he will guide you to all truth [...]"(John 16:12-13).

Only decisions can change your life – this has been our motto for many years. We keep telling people that courage is not a virtue that takes the place of fear. Courage coexists with fear. Charging in with "all guns blazing" and not feeling any fear is not courageous, but foolhardy. Courage is feeling fear, overcoming it, and not retreating. It is precisely this attitude that we need for personal growth.

We have already said that the FALSE SELF is its own kind of counterfeit real identity, and that genuine, healthy relationships are either not possible, or at best very difficult, on the FALSE SELF level. Growth or therapy can be understood as that false structure within us gradually disintegrating. We have to understand that we can contribute to this disintegration (opting for suffering that fosters personal growth, for example, by intentionally choosing situations discomforting to the FALSE SELF) or we can curb and even prevent it by protecting the illusions of life. This is precisely what Jesus was talking about.

There is virtually an infinitude of strategies for smashing our instinctive reactions, just as there are virtually an unlimited number of defense mechanisms. If I am scared of someone, or simply cannot stand him, then I'll sit down right next to him. If I am pathologically jealous of someone, I will not let myself check up on him, and will let him go and have fun, even though I did not choose it. If I have a tendency to constantly tidy up and I never give myself any free time, then I'll leave the dishes in the sink and read for an hour. If I'm always comparing myself to someone and competing with him, then I'll credit him publicly, and tell him what I envy about him. If I have a problem with speaking in public, then I'll volunteer as a lector at Mass. If I am dependent on someone, I'll contact him once a day at the most. If I'm excessively perfecting my appearance, I'll try to go out without makeup. If I cannot refuse myself anything, I'll go to a shop, try on nice clothes, and purchase nothing. I'll enroll in a dancing course, if I have an unresponsive body. If I shield myself by joking incessantly, then I'll go on a retreat in silence for a week. If I'm always silent, then I'll be the first to start talking to people at a party. If I have an assortment of things to do, I'll start with those that are most difficult. I will find a way. **It is important to determine how best to adapt that way to the structure of my FALSE SELF.**

VII.

CHANGES

The next method for actively smashing the FALSE SELF is to make changes. Before we discuss this, however, we need to spend a moment on psychological systems theory.

LIKE IT OR NOT, WE ARE ALL PART OF A STRUCTURE THAT CAN BE CALLED A SYSTEM.

We all belong to many systems. A system might be created by all the citizens of a country, the workers in a company, a retreat group, the members of a community, etc. One of the most important systems to which we belong is the family. We all have our own specific intellectual system in our minds and this also exerts a profound influence on us. Our internal system is the beliefs and opinions we hold as a result of our experiences, the people we meet, our surroundings, and our culture. We (Monika and Marcin) would probably not be Roman Catholics had we been born in Tibet. That is worth bearing in mind.

We would now like to cite a few laws of systems theory, as these are of interest in the context of personal growth.

LAWS OF SYSTEMS THEORY:
1. SYSTEM COMPONENTS ARE
   MUTUALLY DEPENDENT.
2. A SYSTEM WILL DEFEND ITSELF
   AGAINST CHANGE.
3. THE WEAKEST COMPONENT
   EXERCISES CONTROL.

1. SYSTEM COMPONENTS ARE MUTUALLY DEPENDENT

A change in one component of a system triggers a greater or lesser change in all the other components. If we wanted to depict this somehow, we could imagine the mechanism of an old clock made up of lots of cogwheels turning at different speeds. Some of the wheels turn quickly, others slowly, but as a rule, none of them are stationary. **The movement of one will always cause the movement of another,** sometimes almost imperceptibly.

2. A SYSTEM WILL DEFEND ITSELF AGAINST CHANGE

The law of mutual dependence would not be so important were it not for the second law, which states that both **a system as a whole and its individual components defend themselves against change. In a word, systems do not like change and do whatever they can to keep doing things "the old way."** Aversion to change is not a conscious choice. The members of a system do not normally realize that they are doing everything they can to ensure that nothing changes.

A family (grandmother, mother, father, and two sons) came to us because of the anxieties that the younger son, whom we shall call Peter, was suffering. They all came in order to help Peter, who had been refusing to attend classes because of a school phobia. We had no reason to doubt the good will of the family members (the system), all of whom were genuinely very worried about Peter.

However, when we examined the issues more closely, we noticed that Peter's parents had been going through a marital crisis for many years and that their marriage was on the brink of collapse. Their concern for Peter was the only thing holding them together. The crisis would definitely deepen if he were to suddenly recover and rid himself of his anxieties. The marriage might well fall apart.

For her part, the grandmother looked after the sick child while the others were at work or school. She was 70 and caring for Peter was her primary task. Looking after the child justified the grandmother's place in the family. If Peter were to recover, the old woman would have nothing to do. Her life might even lose meaning.

Finally, his brother Paul was obviously "enjoying his freedom." Nobody bothered with him too much. He could sit in front of the computer for hours, while the entire family was dealing with his brother's anxiety attacks. He obviously lacked the attention of his mother and father, but he didn't realize it. If Peter were to recover, Paul's situation might have deteriorated (in his subjective view), because he would suddenly have someone to keep an eye on him.

As for Peter, he was enjoying luxury. So long as everyone was worried about him, he was constantly the center of attention. He only had to feel worse to have everyone by his side. He was subtly manipulating the people around him. He was the most powerful member of the family and he was not going to relinquish that power without a fight. He likewise had no interest in recovering.

3.   THE WEAKEST COMPONENT EXERCISES CONTROL

We can see from this example that, although everybody consciously wants change, they unconsciously fight it. The family described above serves to illustrate the third law: **The weakest component of the system exercises the greatest control over it and holds it together; that is, it stabilizes the system and shields it from change.** Not convinced? Take the case of a newborn. We probably all agree that a completely helpless newborn is the weakest component in the family system. However, a great many issues are "decided" by him: the house has to be rearranged; someone has to get up in the middle of the night; work plans have to be changed; holidays cannot be spent at the usual place. All because of him. For the weakest component, he has a lot of say.

If your family has members who are chronically ill or disabled, or who arouse sympathy, worry, or concern, remember that they have the greatest impact on the system. They decide a lot of things and hold the family members on emotional leashes of various kinds - beginning with feelings of guilt, moving on to concern, and ending with sympathy. This might not happen consciously, but it does happen.

> IF WE WANT TO GROW OR RECOVER,
> OUR PERSONAL GROWTH WILL BRING
> CHANGES THAT WILL NOT BE
> WELCOMED BY THE SYSTEM IN WHICH
> WE FIND OURSELVES.

If we change, then all the other components of the system have to change something. We only agree to change with great difficulty too. Change is associated with crisis, which is generally not pleasant. We have to contend with difficult emotions, such as anxiety, sadness, uncertainty, and sometimes anger. It is not surprising that our change inconveniences everyone else. However, **without change, and therefore without a crisis, there is no maturity or personal growth.** Avoiding change will hold us in place. We cannot move forward unless we open up to change and embrace the crisis associated with it.

> FEAR OF CHANGE IS THE ENEMY OF
> PERSONAL GROWTH.

Marcin: When I was a little boy, I planted a chestnut in a flowerbed, and to my great joy, it grew into a sapling that sprouted two leaves. I was curious to see what would happen next year. Would my chestnut tree grow? As it happened, there were two leaves again the second year, but the sapling looked miserable. The leaves ended up being gnawed by my hamster. So ended the sad life of the flowerbed chestnut tree.

This story appears before my eyes when I look at some people's lives. Some people avoid difficult feelings at all costs and never enter into a crisis situation. Their lives become dwarfed and they fail to live up to the best of their abilities. It is as if something were holding them back.

The classic example is the fear of leaving home. Grown children can rationalize living with their parents into their forties with any number of logical arguments. The more intelligent they are, the more logical the reasons they can devise to justify to themselves that the flowerbed is the best place to live.

I'm not convinced by arguments along the lines of "Living with my parents means I can save up to buy my own home." In most of the cases I know of, these people have somehow saved and saved without accumulating anything. Then there is the argument that the parents cannot be left alone because they are infirm. And they really are becoming like this with children at home. They just might be more active and agile if they didn't have a child around. Who knows?

*I remember how, when I packed my backpack and went to find a room with a lonely old woman in exchange for doing the shopping and keeping the stove burning, I found my first self-contained space. Nobody held a gun to my head. I could have kept living with my parents. However, I wanted to try living on my own before getting married. I have to say that it was not comfortable. It was obviously **considerably less comfortable** than living with my parents, but **that was the price of maturity and freedom**. If a student not earning a regular income could move away from home, then so* *can a working person. The only question is whether he really wants to.*

Obviously, circumstances vary and we cannot generalize, but a lot of people hamper their personal growth by staying at home with their parents.

Some people are in a chronic crisis precisely because they refuse to open themselves up to change. The new is unpredictable: there is no telling what is going to happen when we make a change. What does this decision lead to? Many people justify the stagnation in their lives with religious arguments. The indecision and inertia in their lives are coated with a "spiritual sauce," and can be excused by their ignorance of the will of God. "If I only knew what God wanted of me, I would definitely do it! But because I still don't know, I'll have to pray and wait." And so they subtly unburden themselves of the responsibility of making decisions by remaining infantile.

One man came to us because he was suffering from depression after breaking up with his fiancée. He left her because he felt that he should have been at a seminary. However, he did not become a seminarian because he felt that he still loved her. And so he had been flailing around for years, seeking the will of God. We told him the following story:

"A knight was preparing to go on a crusade in order to fight an enemy. He had a wonderful suit of armor, sword, horse, and squire. He cut quite a figure in his full panoply. He just couldn't decide which war to set off for. East or west? He finally decided on set off for the east. At the end of his first day of travelling, the following thought came to him as he was seated near the evening fire: "What if God wants me to go west and fight? Perhaps I should go there? Maybe I'm more needed there?" After a sleepless night, he told his squire: "We're going back, we're heading west." And so they set off. At the end of their first day's march, he sat by the evening fire and thought: "Perhaps I'd be of more use in the east after all. That may be what God wants of me. I want to serve Him faithfully, so we'll head

off in the opposite direction in the morning." And so it went on for years. The knight grew old and no longer had the strength to raise his sword. His squire had left him and his suit of armor had gone rusty. Despite having everything he needed, he had not fought in a single battle. He thought he was seeking the will of God, but in reality, he was afraid. The knight was scared to fight. He was guided by concern to save his own skin, and, as a result of his perfectionism, he was scared of making a mistake."

__God is indifferent to which good you choose, but it is important that you make a choice to devote your life to someone or something.__ Listen to your desires. If they have been cleansed, then God speaks through them.[76] Act this way and you will never fail to discern the will of God, as trust, not infallibility, is key here. The main thing is that you take up the fight.

Our patient went back to his fiancée when he heard this story. Luckily for him, she took him back and they are now a happy couple.

While the difficulty of making a decision might be apparent when it involves changing something patently immature for something more developed, or something bad for something better, **abandoning something that is good for something else that is good requires genuine courage.** How much light and determination are needed when following the Voice that wants to take us further. Those around us will be marshalled in defense of the status quo: "What are you doing? Isn't your life good the way it is? What's gotten into you? This is some sort of fad you are chasing! Or, could it be the devil talking?"

We once went to a theater to see a 3D nature film describing life in the Amazon rainforest. The main character was a plump caterpillar. We observed its life from the moment it was hatched. The caterpillar was green, and spent its entire life eating leaves that were

---

[76] By "cleansed" we mean that your desires are not the result of your selfishness or covetousness, and that they are in line with the Church's teaching on morality.

just as green as it was. Its whole purpose in life could be summed up as eating green leaves and excreting green waste. It was surrounded by thousands of others like it similarly occupied. Living and not dying – a picture of complete happiness and fulfilment. The leaves were plentiful, but for some unknown reason, the caterpillar began to act strangely at a certain point. It started doing a mysterious dance, secreting mucus, and enveloping itself, until it was completely enclosed and immobile in an ugly black cocoon. The action of the film came to a halt, as there was nothing to show. The cocoon was not particularly attractive. We could imagine the others saying: "Look! What's up with her? What on earth has gotten into that weirdo? Everyone knows that respectable caterpillars don't behave like that! A respectable caterpillar is green, eats green leaves, and poops green poop. We don't need anything else. That cocoon is awful! Didn't we tell you she would end badly?"

And then came the miracle. You obviously know what happened, and although it was expected, all of us in the cinema were rendered numb with the sensation of having participated in a mystery. An enchanting butterfly flew out of the cocoon. Even though it had the same DNA, it was hard to believe that it was the same creature. It was stunning, it was colourful, and it was soaring high. An innocent nature film created a mystical atmosphere – the audience was watching it as if they were spellbound.

If Francesco Bernadone had not left his father's shop, he would have been one of the thousands of rich merchants, and we would never have heard of St. Francis of Assisi. If a certain sister from Kolkata had not decided to reach out to the poor beyond the walls of her congregation, she would have fulfilled her teaching duties to rich girls admirably. If we cannot summon the courage to change when the time is right, then we might remain decent people, whereas we were meant to be saints.

To abandon a good for a greater good is not easy and we should not do so without first making sure that we are not deluded. We should check whether we are being faithful to the Church and to our own previously adopted calling. Change does not interrupt the sure continuity and logic of the personal growth achieved so far: While a butterfly is not in the least similar to a caterpillar, it continues to have the same genetic code. A call to change has to be distinguished from an escape from a hard place, where we should perhaps persist despite our despondency. It is worth submitting to some authority that does not belong to our system so as not to succumb to subjectivsm. This sometimes means changing our community, abandoning something that has hitherto nourished us, worked well, and borne fruit. Some are called to change jobs, others to take up a whole new field of study. Sometimes we are called by grace to move far away, change our environment, and leave our friends and acquaintances.

How often do we become, not servants of God, but of an image of Him which we have created according our own requirements. We defend organizations and structures thinking that we are defending truth or orthodoxy. It is worth checking whether our heart is being broadened. Is my consciousness, my love, embracing an ever wider orbit, and thereby becoming increasingly catholic (i.e. universal)? Could I be ossifying in a moribund framework of ritual and organization, mistaking faithfulness and submission with mindlessness and passivity? The Holy Spirit is an eternally new wine,[77] and new wine is poured into new wineskins.[78] **Unless we open ourselves up to change in thinking about God, the Church, our community, and our inner life, we could well end up spending our entire life faithful to the skins and not the wine.**

---

[77] Cf. Acts 2:13.

[78] Cf. Luke 5:38.

VIII.

TYPOLOGY OF PERSONALITIES

Remember that we first have to know ourselves if we are going to act effectively to smash the FALSE SELF. The typology of personalities, detailed in the table below, may be of assistance here.[79]

The first column has the numbers and types of personalities, which are given symbolic names. We would like to emphasize that there are no good or bad personalities. None of them are more or less preferred. Each carries generic risks, but each also submits to grace, and contributes an irreplaceable coloring and gift to the human family. For particular types, we have given examples of saints, who can be considered representative of their given personality.

The second column shows the personality's dominant aptitudes, gifts, and attributes. These can become part of a person's charm, but they can also develop into a caricature of a virtue. For example, someone who loves orderliness and rules can do an excellent job of organizing community life. She can, however, also become insufferably meticulous to everyone around her if her FALSE SELF defense mechanisms take over.

The third column shows the main sin and the faults that lie at the roots of most of the sins of people with the given personality type. This is interesting and important information, because most people

---

[79] This is largely based on The Enneagram: A Christian Perspective by Richard Rohr and Andreas Elbert (Polish title: *Enneagram. Dziewięć typów osobowości, published by WAM*).

struggle with sin fairly superficially, and have no idea where the ax of self-development needs to be applied to the FALSE SELF.

The fourth column lists the defense mechanisms deployed by the FALSE SELF of the given personality type. We therefore propose areas and orientations for inner work for each personality type in the final column.

Personal growth leads to fullness in Christ: Every saint, regardless of personality type, who does not quit, becomes similar to Jesus and thus to other saints as well. Jesus' personality contains every personality type – all fully developed and integrated in perfect harmony. This typology, as with any schema, orders and clarifies, but it can also become a temptation. We caution against excessively schematising yourself, and especially others. You might see traits or mechanisms characteristic of several disparate personality types in yourself. Let each take what seems useful to himself. Although we are seeking light for our own life, typology also helps us better understand those around us.[80]

[80.]Typology should not be used with the very young. It is our view that people aged 20 and under should not be shown their defense mechanisms. This is obviously not to say that young people should not make a conscious effort to grow. Quite the opposite. It simply means that the starting point for self-development for a young person should not be typology, but rather, in love, getting him to see his own faults and shortcomings, as well as the needs of the world around him.

Personality Type	Gifts and Endowments	Deadly sins, temptations, and shortcomings	Defense Mechanisms	Means of smashing the FALSE SELF
TYPE I **Idealist** (Saint Ignatius of Loyola)	Yearns to be exemplary and improve the world, and for the world to be just and moral. Mobilizes others. Oriented towards success and achieving results. Multitalented. Skilled at systematizing and record keeping. Seeks purity. Thrifty and economical. Loves order. Prompt and punctual. Strong powers of persuasion.	**Anger** - Often repressed, as it is humiliating and ineffective to try to persuade the Idealist. Perfectionism. Workaholism. Despotism. Authoritarianism. Tightly holds onto power. Inability to accept imperfection in oneself or others. Inflexibility of thought and action. Scrupulosity and legal rigor. Constant activity and feeling pressed for time. Overly serious and no sense of humour. Over-sensitivity to criticism. Sexual compulsion (addictive personality). Vindictiveness to the point of making notes of other people's mistakes.	Controlled responses expressed in a peculiar emotional rigidity. Self-censorship of feelings, especially anger. Activity as a defense mechanism The idealist hides behind serving people, gainful employment, evangelizing, etc. If religiosity is a fixed part of his defense mechanisms, then he can paradoxically be restricted by it. Endlessly refining details. Avoiding people who think and act differently. Avoiding criticism. Clamming up and insulting; sulking. Acting on the "all or nothing" principle. Depression. This is obviously an illness in its own right, but for the Idealist it is often a form of escape, in which sense it can be understood as a defense mechanism.	Ceasing activity is a prerequisite. Be aware of our aggressive attitudes (tapping our anger and not disavowing it). Reconcile yourself to your weaknesses (uncover them, talk about them publicly, joke about yourself and "your" works). Accept that neither the world nor your friends and family are perfect (be open to communing with imperfection, accept crude, imperfect solutions, trust in Providence). Delegating power is essential; enduring "bad management." Understand our own subjectivity. Be open to people who think differently and consider their opinions, understand that the destination can be reached by many different roads. Disputes between accuser and accused often play out inside the Idealist's head. These must be observed, halted and resolved in a manner compassionate to him (and for his benefit). Try saying: "I made a mistake," "I was wrong," etc. Repeat: "The world already has a Savior; I don't need

PersonalityType	Gifts and Endowments	Deadly sins, temptations, and shortcomings	Defense Mechanisms	Means of smashing the FALSE SELF
				to worry about anything." Break up the sulk. It is especially important to keep making contact with people who have somehow let the Idealist down. Seek the companionship of people who often joke and have a good sense of humor. Stop trying to fix the world, have more fun, and enjoy life. Commune with nature. Contemplation (passivity, acceptance, enduring our imperfection during silent prayer..
TYPE II **Volunteer** (Saint Teresa of Calcutta)	Prepared to sacrifice oneself for others. Duty and dedication. Concerned about feelings of others. Appreciates and support others. Ability to smile and be pleasant for others. Capacity for empathy and the ability to sense what is required..	**Feeling of superiority** - mostly unconscious. Emotionally recharged by the gratitude of family and friends. Expectation of quid pro quo (praise, better treatment, distinction). Frustration, and even aggression, when assistance not accepted. Exploitation of service to obtain an important position in a group. Feeling indispensable and irreplaceable. Independence. Indebted to nobody. Savior of the world. Styled on "Mother Teresa of Calcutta." Propensity to enter neurotic unions: I	Serving others becomes a form of earning love and approval. Building the FALSE SELF through dedicating oneself to others. Controlling others by serving them. It is hard to refuse someone to whom we feel indebted. Helping others and always doing something is a means of escape from one's own problems. Maintaining emotional independence through reluctance to accept assistance.	Every once in a while, neglect activities for others and switch to acceptance. Enjoy moments of pleasure and relaxation. Learn to be with others and to be alone. The Volunteer is seldom completely alone or completely present to others. Ask others for assistance as an exercise, even in trivial matters where you can manage perfectly well unaided. Disclose weaknesses in front of others. Discover your needs, respond to

PersonalityType	Gifts and Endowments	Deadly sins, temptations, and shortcomings	Defense Mechanisms	Means of smashing the FALSE SELF
		(supportive and redeeming) vs. You (dependent and addicted). Personal neglect that can result in accident or illness. Spontaneous disavowal of praise, and denial of achievements and strengths. Religious and communal life or service can foster neurotic behavior.		them, and fulfil them through things like hobbies and sports. Do not be ashamed of personal needs, especially sensual and emotional ones. In particular, get involved in aid activities that are unseen and anonymous. Learn to say no. Accept praise without comment, especially if this is difficult. Contemplation: passivity and acceptance, receiving God's love.
TYPE III **Leader** (Pope Saint John Paul II)	Competent and gifted. Ability to adjust to surroundings and circumstances, and immediately grasp the expectations of others. Acting talent. Leading and organizing talent. Strong powers of persuasion. Clearly defined goals. Inspires others to become active, enters into the spirit of the community. Driven to succeed. Sees projects through effectively and efficiently. Pursues personal growth.	**Lying** - intended to inflate results, hide failures, achieve victories, and create impressions. Building the FALSE SELF by inducing admiration. Seeking praise. Showboating. Posturing and dramatizing. Impetuosity and aggression. Desire to get one's own way at all costs. Aggression towards anyone who can threaten success or steal the limelight. Delusions of grandeur. Resistance to authority, especially in areas where the Leader operates. Conveying an impression of	Achieving success is an edifice of the FALSE SELF, feeding off the admiration of those around us. Activity, even noble activity, can be antithetical to personal growth in this case. Accommodating the expectations of those around us to be noticed. There are as many versions of the FALSE SELF as there are environments. She will be the quietest one on the retreat, the loudest one in the pub, etc. Deceiving ourselves and others on our real skills and actual motivations. Hiding the weak points of our proposals. Can convince ourselves anything is	Catch each lie you tell (even the slightest bending of the facts), and expose it to yourself and others. Be aware of your real motives. Admit to ignorance, mistakes, failures, and incompetence. Speak highly of authorities and competitors. Avoid situations in which you might appear as the star. Do not boast of achievements, stay in the background, behind your co-workers. Do not talk about yourself. Listen to what others have to say. Try to say "I don't know, I know nothing about that".

Personality Type	Gifts and Endowments	Deadly sins, temptations, and shortcomings	Defense Mechanisms	Means of smashing the FALSE SELF
		competence on every topic.	true, so long as others acknowledge that we are right, when in fact we are wrong. Acting in a way that maintains an image that people will like.	Do not hold forth on every topic, no matter how strong the temptation to do so. Learn to be alone and keep quiet. Be yourself and do not adjust yourself to meet the expectations of those around you. Do not respond to criticism. Listen to it in its entirety and try to see the critic's viewpoint, even against your will. See your misfortunes as blessings in disguise. Compete in areas in which you are not proficient, thereby exposing yourself to losing. Periods of inactivity – R&R – are a must. Contemplation: accept yourself with distractions, acknowledge lapses of concentration, embrace hidden life.
TYPE IV **Artist** (Saint Francis of Assissi)	Love of beauty. Artistic talents. Skilled at interacting through feelings. Sensitivity to and understanding of emotional life. A need for emotional sensations. Great deal of emphasis on original dress and behavior.	**Jealousy and comparison** - constant striving to be the most authentic. Provocative or scandalous behavior. Yielding to emotions in relationships and inner life. Frequent shame/embarrassment, sometimes unconscious. Rejection of societal norms.	Being unconventional and noticed – in the service of the FALSE SELF. Mortal fear of being rejected or laughed at. Being ourselves by standing out from those around us: constantly living relative to others. Hiding behind extravagant behavior and outfits, sometimes humorously.	Personal growth can be difficult for the Artist, as he associates being like everyone else with losing his own personality. He has to understand this in order to mature. Periods of being "oneself" (days of silence where there is no show to put on for anyone) are indispensable. Expose yourself to the ordinary, the normal, and the

PersonalityType	Gifts and Endowments	Deadly sins, temptations, and shortcomings	Defense Mechanisms	Means of smashing the FALSE SELF
	Overwhelming need to "be oneself." Romanticism.	Losing oneself in constantly creating personal image. Flamboyant attire is an indispensable part of this. Giving in to sadness or depression; feelings from which an artist can derive a certain pleasure. Thoughts of death. Repugnance at one's own body and appearance. Fear of "ordinary" family life. Hypersensitivity and emotional instability, yielding to extreme moods, from mania to depression.	Independence misconstrued as an expression of personal freedom. Dramatizing one's unhappy state. Theatrical behavior due to deriving satisfaction from the interest of others. Playing out dramas for ourselves. Artists can try so hard to discover their authenticity that they actually become artificial, sometimes grotesquely so to those around them.	everyday. Stand in line, despite possibly getting the subjective impression of betraying yourself. One of the worst statements for the Artist's FALSE SELF is "Once you've taken off these fripperies and feathers you're decked out in, you're just like everyone else: ORDINARY." The Artist should repeat this sentence every now and then. Comply with regulations, principles, and norms such as traffic regulations and prayer rules. Be guided in life by faithfulness to resolutions, and not impulses of the heart. There is a particular need to stolidly endure routine and banality. The tension this provokes must be withstood. Discipline and asceticism leads the Artist to maturity. Genuinely commit to serving others. Contemplation: unemotionally and in adherence to the rules.
TYPE V Recluse-Scholar (Edith Stein aka Saint Teresa	Understanding of inner life issues. Love of silence and solitude. Disposed towards a contemplative and mystic life.	Covetousness (greed) - concerning inner life and personal growth, knowledge, ideas, silence, learning, and personal space. Escapism.	Isolation is the basic Type V defense mechanism. Pseudo-mysticism. Pseudospirituality. Suppressing and hiding emotional reactions.	Form close relationships with people (share experiences, fears, difficulties, and especially feelings - something the Recluse finds unbearable).

Personality Type	Gifts and Endowments	Deadly sins, temptations, and shortcomings	Defense Mechanisms	Means of smashing the FALSE SELF
Benedicta of the Cross)	Given to philosophizing. Distance and impartiality towards human affairs. Investigating and uncovering rules and principles. Ingenuity. Attention to detail. Facility for innovative and unorthodox thinking. Open-mindedness. Openness to different cultures, religions, and traditions. Propensity to collect. Complete dedication to passion(s) (such as an area of knowledge, academic research, or inner life). Attracted to asceticism. Thrift. Attentive listening.	Isolation that results in loneliness. Participation in human relationships and affairs solely through observation and intellect. Psychologizing. Aversion to the feelings of others; The Recluse-Scholar often views the expression of feelings as distasteful, unnecessary, or scandalous. Feeling superior to others. Living in an imaginary inner world. Pedantry. "My home is my castle" attitude. Detachment from the real good of others. Pursuit of academic goals with no regard to the human costs. Despotism. Excessively analytical of one's own experiences. Receiving outweighs giving.	Aggression whenever anyone enters your enclosure. Solitude as a place of escape (open to Buddhism, which can be a dead-end for personal growth). Withdrawal. Compartmentalization of personal life, relationships, and feelings.	Become attuned to the emotional reactions of others; do not flee them, and do not hold emotional people in contempt. Be open to spontaneous and unpredictable behavior, touch other people (e.g. contact with children, handicapped people), take up dancing. Get involved in social, political, and religious affairs. Learn love by responding to the needs of others. Defer to the group, enter unions. Overcome the temptation to remain silent and be the first to start talking, try to maintain relationships of deep friendship. Share thoughts, ideas, and discoveries. Maintain contact with the suffering through hospices or aid organizations. Meditate on the Passion of Jesus and His sacrifice for others.
TYPE VI Law-abiding (Saint Josemaría Escrivá de Balaguer)	Loyalty and faithfulness. Capacity for cooperation and compliance. Full commitment to causes believed in.	**Lack of trust in, and fear of, the** **world and of God** – This lack of trust governs much of the activity of the immature but law-abiding. A fear of God and of death can paradoxically	Identifying with a group or a cause is a defense mechanism that absolves us from responsibility for our own decisions and diminishes anxiety. Exercise of religion can cause serious conflict for the	Be aware of your anxiety and aggressive attitudes – start to trust in God and His Providence. Meet people who think differently: those of unfamiliar political party or

PersonalityType	Gifts and Endowments	Deadly sins, temptations, and shortcomings	Defense Mechanisms	Means of smashing the FALSE SELF
	Strong group identification. Preparedness to defend values held with conviction. Forthrightness. Orthodoxy.	be a factor that influences above-average religious commitment, but it is neurotic religiosity thus fuelled by fear. Binary functionality: little flexibility in thought and deed. Distrust of those who think differently, suspicion, and, in extreme cases, attack. Fear means that defense of a group or value (such as patriotism, truth, freedom, or one's nation) is dominated by often unconscious aggression. Scrupulosity, being in thrall to the law, rigorism, and fundamentalism. Tendency for obsessive thinking, to the point of OCD. Mindlessly obedient and compliant. At risk of joining cults and authoritarian religious communities, and feeling fantastic in a clearly defined world where everything is black or white. Seeking and idolizing, while at the same time fearing and despising, an authority figure or guru. Withdrawn and fearful, or aggressively despotic. Cowardice or recklessness.	development of this sense of being law-abiding. Uniformity of thought and action. Projecting own distrustful and aggressive attitude to the world onto others. Ascribing one's own unconscious anxieties to others).	faction, different religion, denomination, worldview, or culture. Risk spontaneous thoughts and actions including religious ones. Cease to control your own or others' actions. Take responsibility for your own life. Realize that the truth can be understood in different ways. Look for non-authoritarian spirituality, where the emphasis is on freedom, leniency, compassion, and childhood. Believe in yourself, do not be afraid of your our own success. Master new skills, train in new areas. Cultivate a sense of humor. Contemplation: non-authoritarian spirituality, trust in our own spiritual experience.
TYPE VII Optimist (Saint Thérèse of Lisieux aka Saint Thérèse of the Child	Positive attitude towards life. Good mood and sense of humor. Given to building communities and offering consolation.	**Inordinately strong attraction to pleasure and shallow optimism** – at the bottom of most of the Optimist's sins. Confuses happiness with pleasure.	Denying problems by pretending that nothing happened. A happy version of the FALSE SELF - one that is difficult to part with.	Expose yourself to the various forms of suffering in the world – commit yourself to bringing genuine relief to the suffering through volunteer

Personality Type	Gifts and Endowments	Deadly sins, temptations, and shortcomings	Defense Mechanisms	Means of smashing the FALSE SELF
Jesus and the Holy Face)	Attracts children. Curiosity regarding the world. Openness to new challenges and experiences. Confidence and optimism. Skill in finding the upside of every situation, no matter how difficult.	Mistakes exterior "peace and quiet" for peace of the heart. Life of the party, always joking. Drawn to a shallow positive spirituality of the "Hallelujah! Praise the Lord!" variety. Avoids the topic of suffering and the cross. Drawn to the Gospel of success. Infantilism. Fixed smile. Prone to exaggeration. Unrestrained in pleasure, eating, and drinking. Addicted to adrenaline.	Avoiding deep relationships out of fear of being rejected and discovering personal sufferings and shortcomings. Postponing difficulties and emotional discomfort, thereby blocking personal development. Interpreting everything to one's own advantage. Shallow spirituality – reaching for what seem to be the fruits of inner life without making any effort.	work, or social and charitable activities. Share your personal sadness, concerns, sufferings, and shortcomings. Do not try to escape from pain. Realize that there is no Easter Sunday without Good Friday. Ponder the Passion of Christ. Force yourself to take up asceticism, fasting, discipline, and regular self-improvement at all costs. Contemplation: faithfulness to committed spiritual practices (such as the Liturgy of the Hours) despite any dryness.
TYPE VIII **Warrior** Catherine of Sienna)	Strength and valor. Sense of justice. Directness and sincerity. Sensitivity to wrongdoing. Responsibility. Reliability. Resilience. Critical approach to reality, that is, to the system in force. Persistence in pursuing goals. Able to motivate others..	**Confrontation and spite** - as a natural response and way of being. **Impurity** - generally understood as exploiting others. Cantankerous, impetuous, violent. Paradoxically uses violence to achieve peace and justice. Enters relationships via confrontation or provocation. Categorizes people as friend or foe. Tough, strong, and resolute in order to survive. Ruthless towards self and others. Severe and disciplined. Vindictive.	Fighting (often for a good cause) is a defense mechanism of the Warrior's FALSE SELF - the Robin Hood trap. Reflexive response of opposition and objection, especially towards competitors and those in authority. Involvement in a sport, politics or some other area associated with conflict can be a trap for the Warrior. Caring for the weak is a common Warrior defense mechanism. However, the weak actually evoke feelings of guilt, anxiety or contempt in the Warrior.	Associate with weak people, not with a view to caring for them or protecting them, but to enter into closer relationships and friendships. Break out of the "Fight the strong, take care of the weak" framework. Share your misconceptions, weaknesses, and mistakes. Display emotion. Defer to someone (for example, in spiritual direction). Break the cycle and receive insight – selfanalysis of motivations; accept your attitudes and feelings.

PersonalityType	Gifts and Endowments	Deadly sins, temptations, and shortcomings	Defense Mechanisms	Means of smashing the FALSE SELF
		Views people as rulers or ruled. Auto-aggression to the point of suicide. Macho man or belligerent feminist..		Learn leniency and compassion, starting with yourself. Observe compulsory days of solitude and silence. Contemplation: leniency and compassion towards yourself.
TYPE IX **Mediator** (Pope Saint John XXIII)	Love of peace and quiet. Seeks equilibrium. Economy of strength, as well as material resources. Ability to relax and unwind. Ability to understand different points of view. Natural mediation ability. Nonabrasiveness. Obedience. Empathy. Universality. Sense of justice.	**Laziness and neglecting** work and other activities – acting only when necessary or when compelled. Energy-efficient living. Lack of ambition. Life stagnation. Subject to anxiety. Skepticism. Untapped talents. No confidence in the success of own actions. Difficulty in making decisions. Aversion to steadily improving in one specific area. Reluctance to assume leadership positions. Unappreciative. Unpredictable outbursts of anger and aggression, mainly towards close friends and family. Sloth.	Withdrawing and not taking the initiative are the Mediator's basic defense mechanisms. Humility and a seductive quietness Self-disparagement. Skipping "from flower to flower" if a commitment or interest is involved. Going with the flow. Avoiding confrontation and competition for fear of failure.	Take the initiative and make changes in life. Believe in your own talent. Get involved in group activities and embrace the functions and positions entrusted to you. Get in touch with your own anger and aggression. Initiate meetings and relationships. Assume responsibility for sustaining acquaintances and friendships. Overcome your aversion to calling, contacting, or meeting new people, officiating. Enter contests of various kinds for the sake of competition. Accept risk. Show your strong side publicly. Contemplation: trust in your charism, accept your own spiritual experience, open up to personal development.

IX.

SELF-LOVE

LOVE OF ONESELF, LOVE OF ONE'S NEIGHBOR, AND LOVE OF GOD ARE INSEPARABLE.

Imagine you categorized the relationships you have with others according to the following template of percentages: "I love: a%, I can tolerate: b%, I'm indifferent to: c%, I avoid or I'm scared of: d%, I don't like: e%, and finally, I hate: f%. Then, you could roughly translate them into your relationship with yourself: "I love this much about myself, I tolerate this much, I'm indifferent to this much, I'm scared of this much, I don't like this much, and finally, I hate this much." You could do the same with your relationship to God and determine the percentages by which I love, accept, fear, or hate Him, and so on. Jesus often disabused those who thought they could love God in heaven, while hating their neighbor. If you cannot forgive someone else, then you cannot forgive yourself. Furthermore, you are carrying a grievance against God. Whoever fears people also is afraid of God, and does not trust his own self.

Jesus identified love of Him with love of others: "...I was in prison, and you visited me."[81] **Genuine love of God is measured by love of others**. But are you aware that this is similarly measured by love of yourself? To not love yourself is to reject the Creator that

---

[81] Cf. Matt 25:36.

gave you life and molded you. Many people unconsciously curse God, exclaiming: "I did not work out for You, You made a mistake, making me like this!" **You cannot love God and your neighbor unless you love yourself.**

WE ONLY HAVE AS MUCH LOVE FOR GOD AND OTHERS AS WE HAVE FOR OURSELVES.
LOVING ONESELF IS THE FIRST NATURAL COMMANDMENT.

People find it hard to understand what a well-conceived love of themselves involves. Some see the pitfall of egotism in it. The term "self love" is often used pejoratively to denote egocentricity. But **unless we love ourselves, we cannot love God or others**.

By rejecting ourselves, we reject the Creator and our brothers and sisters. Just as Jesus, the Word "came to what was his own"[82] and was rejected by "his own" we also can reject the Messiah, the Divine Presence, by rejecting ourselves. Just as it was hard for the Jews to believe that one among them was God, it is hard for us to believe that God is "I am". The name of God simultaneously defines our existence.

Is that not miraculous? **God comes to you through you.** Although humans do not have a divine nature and need a Savior, grace speaks through their interior. Until you accept yourself, you also reject the Messiah. All roads lead to the interior. **The beginning of our inner life is our relationship with the REAL SELF within us, the connection and bond with ourselves.** The REAL SELF becomes God through participation in God, according to St. John of the Cross.

---

[82] Jn. 1:11.

The difficulty Jesus' contemporaries had in accepting His mission is similar to the difficulty we have in accepting ourselves: "Such an imperfect, weak, sinful, and lost 'self' was meant to be a vessel in which God would reveal Himself? Can that be taken on faith?" Being faithful to God means being faithful to ourselves and vice versa. The will of God is not something outside us, but is expressed by the stirring of our heart.

A lot of people do not realize that **a deeply ingrained self-aversion is a copy of the aversion that people around us, such as parents, siblings, and others (relationships with schoolmates are especially important here), had towards us when we were children**. It is actually the aversion that the FALSE SELF has towards the REAL SELF. The FALSE SELF has a tendency to become an internal prosecutor against frail love-hungry creatures such as us. We hide our REAL SELF behind increasingly elaborate camouflage, because we are ashamed of ourselves.

In this context, the gospel scene where Jesus wants to hug children, while his disciples brusquely forbid them from approaching the Master, can speak to us in a new way.[83] We can relate the texts in which Jesus identifies with a child, saying that whoever received the child automatically received Him,[84] to our own inner selves. We are that repelled child. The FALSE SELF brusquely forbids him from approaching Jesus. The FALSE SELF is full of criticism and rejection: "I reject that look, that character, those skills." The FALSE SELF is disappointed with the child's weakness and sensitivity, and is ashamed of him. We need to bring this child to Jesus and let Him hug him – to see ourselves as we lean over him and protect him from those who have harmed him. We need to feel pity towards ourselves and anger towards those who have hurt us.

[83.]Cf: Mark 10:13-14.

[84.]Cf. Luke 9:48.

Self-love is expressed through solidarity with our inner child. This is not about imprudently and narcissistically denying our own weakness (disowning our mistakes, failures, defects, and shortcomings is essentially a failure to accept the child within), but about tenderly bowing over ourselves until we feel kindness towards the fragile person that we are. **Only we can care for ourselves properly**. It is surprising how many people can list all the wrongs they have suffered in childhood in monotonous detail without noticing that they themselves are currently tormenting the child they carry within themselves.

If God and His grace are going to be revealed to us, they will be revealed through this child. God is incarnated anew as it were. He has been growing inside us since baptism, which is a sort of Christmas. The REAL SELF grows through the miraculous life of grace until the communal activity of Jesus commences and we are capable of spending our (that is, His) life loving our brothers. "... yet I live; no longer I, but Christ lives in me..." says St. Paul.[85] Unless the child within accepts Jesus, the mystery of God will not be able to be realized through our life.

Therefore, let's try to see ourselves as a child who was not properly loved. Let's recall those painful moments when we were rejected, laughed at, and abandoned. Those moments when we cried and nobody hugged us and wiped away our tears. The horrible shame when we were stigmatized and nobody came to hug us and say: "Everything's going to be all right, we've been waiting for you." Let's remember not being accepted and all the times when we were overwhelmed by the vastness of evil, not knowing how to react to it. Perhaps someone we trusted transgressed our physical or psychological boundaries. Let's recall those unpleasant moments when our parents were hurting one another, and each was trying to

---

[85] Gal. 2:20

draw us into an alliance against the other with the ultimatum: "It's either me or him/her." Let's call to mind all those times when we heard footsteps on the stairs and didn't know whether to run to meet them or run away. Let's recall the child we were – helpless, embarrassed, humiliated, not fully understanding what was happening, betrayed, and forsaken. And let's try to lean over him. Let's protect, console, and hug him. Let's definitely take him away from those places where he was hurt or wronged. Let us do so resolutely, with a heart full of tenderness and heartfelt love. Let us see that Jesus identifies with this weak child. "Amen I say to you, unless you turn and become like children, you will not enter the kingdom of heaven."[86] Let's persist, then, in consolation in knowing that grace will come to us along this road. If need be, let's look back to that picture over and over until the persecution of that which is most fragile in us ceases, the embarrassment wears off, and confidence in and kindness towards ourselves emerge.

We once spoke with a man who had suffered a great deal in childhood at the hands of his alcoholic parents. When we invoked the picture of the child, he understood that he taken the baton from his childhood tormentors and was now his own torturer, and that he was keeping the boy he once was in a closet, as he was ashamed to show him to the world. (He was pathologically shy.) He understood that he despised his inner child but decided to put a stop to it. This was a make-or-break moment. He decided to take this boy to all the places where he was ashamed (i.e. he would go where he was ashamed to go as an adult, as he would feel like a lesser person); that he would never let go of his hand and would never leave him alone. He was angry towards his FALSE SELF, because he realized that he had let himself be deceived for many years and had been defending a fake image. From that moment on, he began to act completely contrariwise. He smashed the FALSE SELF and

---

[86] Matt 18:3. That is, unless we accept the child within.

supported the child. He felt God reveal Himself through his inner child not long afterwards.

If we started to love ourselves, we would start to take care of ourselves.

We would take care of our bodies. We would treat them with due respect and acceptance. Once we understood that the body is transitory and that it is the temporary abode of the soul, we would provide it with what it truly needs. We would understand that any deficiencies in love of our own bodies are deficiencies in love for ourselves.[87] If we loved our bodies, then we would keep them clean, dress well, and see to it that we had a pleasant fragrance and that our hair was combed. We would treat our bodies gently once we noticed that they're not perfect and that they age. We would allow them to rest while taking care of their fitness.

We would take care of our emotional needs. We would see to it that our bodies were furnished with warmth, love, and beauty by maintaining close and pure relationships with our friends, and through art and elegant candlelit meals. We would avoid living in a rush and always being busy. We would let ourselves squander a little time and money out of self-love. We would smear expensive relaxation oil on ourselves, and we would do so without feeling guilty. We would cherish these joyful moments in the knowledge that this is also how self-love is realized. Pleasure would not be redundant or something to be avoided at all costs. We would remember that, although pleasure in itself is not happiness, we still need it for emotional balance, and we would make sure that we had some relaxation time occasionally. We would distinguish living for pleasure from reasonable enjoyment for our own good.

---

[87] Some people are excessively concerned about their health and appearance, and panic when they start to age, but this is more a symptom of lack of acceptance of the order of creation than of love for oneself.

We would distinguish egocentrism and laziness from legitimately caring for ourselves. We would be gentle and patient with ourselves, and ordinarily good. We would approach our limitations and shortcomings with humor, while understanding the need for personal growth. **We would set ourselves requirements, but without violence or self-aggression**. We would stand in truth, seeing the beauty manifested within us and the good that passes through us, while admitting to our imperfections. By accepting our weakness in this manner, we would become humble and charitable.

Some people find self-development that involves resting or allowing themselves a little pleasure very strenuous. They are compulsive doers, and inactivity (which is what they understand by "resting") makes them tense and even anxious. Unless they understand that their activity is in large measure driven by their defense mechanisms, they will be trapped, occasionally doing a lot of good for others to their own detriment.

Others suffer an enormous burden of guilt when they afford themselves something pleasant. Similarly, they need to understand that an aversion to pleasure is not a manifestation of inner freedom or love of poverty, but has its origins in the FALSE SELF.

We need to be on guard against confusing legitimate concern for personal growth with a perfectionism that compels incessant activity. The purpose of personal growth is not perfection, but love. When Jesus exhorts us to be perfect, he does so in the context of God's mercy: "So be perfect, just as your heavenly Father is perfect,"[88] which means "Let your heart be as wide as His heart," and "Be merciful, just as your Father is merciful."[89]

The opposite of perfectionism is not chaos, but mercy. While perfectionism feeds on fear and a lack of self-acceptance, mercy results from love and confidence. Perfectionism brings tension,

---

[88] Cf. Matt 5:48.

[89] Cf. Luke 6:36.

rivalry, and violence. Mercy engenders gentleness, cooperation, and peace. Perfectionism causes division and disappointment. Mercy produces communion and understanding.

	PERFECTIONISM	MERCY
IS BORN OF:	FEAR SELF-REJECTION	CONFIDENCE SELF-LOVE
BRINGS:	TENSION RIVALRY VIOLENCE	GENTLENESS COOPERATION PEACE
PRODUCES	DIVISION REJECTION DISAPPOINTMENT	COMMUNION ACCEPTANCE UNDERSTANDING

Since we have to be someone, we should be ourselves. We cannot cloak ourselves in the holiness of Jesus by rejecting ourselves. "Jesus, I trust in You" cannot be put into practice without trusting ourselves and those we love.

X.

LOVE FOR OUR FELLOW HUMAN BEINGS
(CONCERN FOR THE GROWTH OF OTHERS)

> DOING GOOD IS FAR MORE IMPORTANT THAN STRIVING FOR PERFECTION.

Suppose we have spent years fighting some weakness that always throws us. We are not suggesting that we give up the fight (especially if the weakness is sinful), but it is worth asking ourselves whether it might not be better to concentrate our efforts on doing something good for someone else. **If we cannot stop doing a certain humiliating thing, we can always start selflessly doing some good for someone else. The fruitfulness of our lives is measured by love, not emotional restraint**. Obviously, this second task is important (because it enables even more love), but it would be a mistake to think that we are incapable of love, as our weakness constantly humiliates us. Self-development decisions can obviously adopt a negative form: "I'm not going to be this, I'm not going to be that." But decisions involving love: "I will be this or that" are far more substantial. **Life is not just about not doing wrong, but mainly about embracing the good**. Soup is not made from recipes written as "Do not add parsley, do not add plums, etc." It's the same with love – **it's not so much about what not to do as what *to do***.

> LOVE DISPENSED SELFLESSLY COMES
> BACK TO US AND AFFECTS OUR
> PERSONAL GROWTH.

This first of all concerns simple deeds that make our neighbor feel loved, appreciated, noticed, cared for, listened to, and understood. The first and perhaps the most important step is to look around and take concrete action, so that those around me feel love. I might think I love them, but how can I actually tell? This is not about what I think, but how those closest to me feel. What would they say if someone were to ask them whether they felt loved by me?

This is also about creating environments and communities brimming with love, where there is no authoritarianism or moralizing, where phrases such as "we have to," "we ought to," "it's our duty," or "we're not allowed to," are not habitually used, and where human weakness is not treated with suspicion.

We need communities in which it is understood that Christianity is not a list of dos and don'ts, or a religion with a wrathful God that must be appeased, but an embracing of the Breath of Life, which makes us freer, happier, and more triumphant. Unless we build simple, poor, and contemplative communities where merciful love is the beginning and end of all activity, people will leave the Church, as they will not see anything of interest in it. "Where the body is, there the vultures will gather"[90] – people hungry for God will spontaneously gather wherever love is manifested in specific deeds and attitudes. There is no need to coerce them into anything, frighten them with anything, or chase them; they will come of their own accord, because everyone is hungry for love.

[90.] Luke 17:37.

Everyone can find their own specific way of loving their neighbor. There are as many options as there are people. I can always do something for someone else, even if I am afflicted with enormous emotional and/or physical shortcomings. **Love is possible at any time and by almost any means.** However, we would like to emphasize a specific aspect of love: leading others to maturity.

> TENDING TO THE PERSONAL GROWTH OF OTHERS IS AN ESSENTIAL ASPECT OF LOVE; ONE THAT AFFECTS OUR OWN PERSONAL GROWTH.

Once we intentionally begin to care for the growth of others by, for example, sharing problems similar to those broached in this book, we will be free of our own FALSE SELF. **Helping yourself while helping others** is a truly extraordinary experience. We are obviously not trying to turn our readers into "amateur therapists," but to encourage them to run workshops, give lectures, or conduct discussion groups or meetings on sharing personal growth and cooperation with grace with the assistance of this or some other book. This book can be used for self-development (which was, after all, why it was written) on its own, in conjunction with others, or in pastoral work. **Conveying knowledge on personal growth is a major component of self-development.** Do not wait until you are recognized as being sufficiently learned and adequately trained.

IF WHAT IS WRITTEN HERE HAS AFFECTED YOU, **COMMUNICATE IT FURTHER AND SHARE WHAT YOU HAVE UNDERSTOOD AND EXPERIENCED OF THE MYSTERIOUS ASSISTANCE OF GRACE.**
GOD SUPPORTS ANY ACTIVITY THAT LEADS PEOPLE TO GREATER LOVE.

The maxim, "To anyone who has, more will be given," holds true.[91] **Obviously, it is necessary to exercise humility and to act as a student, not a teacher.** We are all useless servants. We need to remain vigilant against "psychologizing" spirituality, while bearing in mind that the truths in the gospels have parallels in psychology. Lights are not placed under bushels. **Every action, even the most simple or trivial, taken to expand the awareness of others is palpably supported "from above" and pays dividends in our own growth in love. It is worth being personally convinced of this.**

---

[91] Luke 8:18.

XI.

LOVE OF GOD (PRAYER)

PRAYER IS THE MOST SIGNIFICANT ACTIVITY THAT CAN BE UNDERTAKEN IN LIFE.

Although this chapter on prayer as the practice of the love of God comes near the end of the book, prayer is far and away **the most significant action that can be taken to be free of the FALSE SELF.** Through prayer, we reach the Source of Life, which is never depleted and, most importantly, which flows from within ourselves, and is therefore independent of external circumstances. Prayer is an acceptance of life. Prayer is the breath that we draw from within. Prayer causes us to regain our sovereignty, so that we do not have to beg anyone for a modicum of attention or affection. Prayer restores our internal freedom, as we cease to be afraid and experience life within ourselves. Thanks to prayer, love begins to be possible.

A wounded person is like a crab encased in the shell of the FALSE SELF. The shell of a crustacean is indispensable to its existence. It is the exoskeleton on which its whole body depends. Nobody in their right mind would give up such a protective shell without receiving something in exchange. An endoskeleton has to be produced before our defense mechanisms can be discarded. **Prayer is what builds this skeleton inside us and makes it possible to shed the outer shell of defense mechanisms. No one who has not** experienced inner life will abandon his pretences. The anxiety is too strong.

As therapists, we have observed that therapy progresses considerably faster when the patient engages in prayer, and especially contemplative prayer.[92] However, what people consider prayer is very often not the real thing. From our standpoint, although the people who come to us are very religious and would unequivocally claim that they prayed, their religious observance does not meet the criterion of "true prayer" as described below. **The study of prayer is often a watershed moment in therapy.**

"Where do the wars and where do the conflicts among you come from? Is it not from your passions that make war within your members? You covet but do not possess. You kill and envy but you cannot obtain; you fight and wage war. You do not possess because you do not ask. You ask but do not receive, because you ask wrongly, to spend it on your passions."[93] These telling words from the Epistle of James should give us pause for thought. **It is worth asking ourselves whether we pray well, but even more, whether this activity, which we occasionally engage in for religious reasons, can be called prayer at all**. We obviously respect every religious gesture, but inner life is subordinate to personal growth. We can introduce the analogous concept of "real prayer" in a similar way as we utilize the concepts of the "real self" and "true thought."

What we have in mind when we say that prayer rapidly accelerates recovery and emotional integration is the **real prayer** that Jesus taught, and not some religious ritual discharged haphazardly, perfunctorily, hurriedly, and with a complete lack of internal commitment, by force of habit, or out of fear or some other

---

[92.]What we have in mind here is acquired contemplation.

[93.]James 4:1-3.

motivation(s), even noble ones such as socio-political ends.[94] Jesus taught that prayer should be "in Spirit and truth."[95] This is the only sort of prayer that will open the individual up to the presence of God and enable him to gradually enter into the miraculous life.

What then is real prayer and what are its attributes? What does it mean to pray well? Let's spend some time pondering these questions.

1.   REAL PRAYER IS ENGAGED IN OUT OF LOVE

The most important reason to engage in prayer is the love of The One to Which we return. **Prayer is not a technique meant to help us through emotional or practical difficulties**. Nor does it appease God, so that He will start to support our life plans and ideas. **Prayer is an acceptance of His Life. We pray because we love Him and want to love Him even more**.

How and what we feel are of no importance when praying. We have no interest in whether our prayer will "work out" for us. When I love, I cease to matter to myself; I only want the good of That Which I love. Prayer begins to gradually free us from ourselves. This also happens through the difficulties we experience while praying. The importance of not assessing our prayer in terms of its efficiency, effectiveness or quality is crucial here. Once our ego vanishes, prayer becomes completely simple and disinterested.

Prayer leads us to a complete acceptance of the ways in which God operates and manifests Himself in our lives. It is not about obtaining something from God, but obtaining God. When we pray, we wish to express our thanks to God for the miraculous grace that

---

[94] Obviously, this does not mean that you cannot pray for your country or social issues. You can and should. However, prayer cannot become a mere tool in a political battle.

[95] "But the hour is coming, and is now here, when true worshippers will worship the Father in Spirit and truth; and indeed the Father seeks such people to worship him. God is Spirit, and those that worship him must worship in Spirit and truth." John 4:23-24.

we have received. The very fact that we seek Him attests to His having found us.

2.   REAL PRAYER IS SINCERE AND DOES NOT REQUIRE VERBOSITY

Sincerity is the cornerstone of prayer. We should not try to be anyone other than who we really are when we pray. **Prayer requires truth.** If we feel anxiety, then we should not pretend that we are confident. If we do not understand what is happening in our life and are feeling pain, then we have the right to "pour out our heart" to God.

Some people start to behave strangely when they pray: they switch to a pompous style, use archaic words, and adopt an unnatural tone of voice. They behave so artificially as to give the impression of playing a role. We have to be ourselves, and not how we think God wants to see us, when we pray. It is better to dispute with God than to feign obedience.

God knows what we need before we even ask Him, so we do not have to explain anything to Him. Oratorical skill is not required to pray well. Beautiful prayers written by others can help, but our own simple words are best. Why? Because they are ours.

3.   REAL PRAYER IS DIRECTED INWARD

When we pray, we do not seek God outside ourselves, but enter our interior, because He abides in the depths of our heart. Internal and external silence thus become a prerequisite of and a pathway to prayer. St. John of the Cross, a great teacher of prayer, put it as follows: "The Father spoke one Word, which was his Son, and this

Word he speaks always in eternal silence, and in silence must it be heard by the soul."[96]

Religious rituals and ceremonies have been instituted to lead us to the interior, where we can find the Presence of God. If they do not serve that purpose, it is because they are poorly discharged or poorly experienced, in which case they become useless, and possibly even harmful. God is closer than we think: "For in him we live, and move, and have our being."[97] **The development of prayer leads us towards perpetual communion with the Personal Love living inside us.**

4. REAL PRAYER INVOLVES THE HEART

If prayer is going to be rea , then it cannot become a catnap, a rest, or a dream. Prayer is always a struggle to keep our heart with God. It presupposes an attitude of vigilance, and this is also expressed in our complete respect for our external demeanor.

We can sometimes find ourselves praying with our body and our lips, while our mind is far away. The distractions we experience when praying perform two important functions. First, they show us our weakness and thereby render us simple and humble. Second, they indicate those parts of our inner self that are still disordered and which can be addressed outside prayer time. All we can do when we pray is to return to the Divine Presence humbly and without stress. Most people reject prayer precisely because they cannot stand themselves.

Prayer requires our whole life to be oriented to the miraculous and the interior. Sometimes this means making drastic decisions

---

[96] St. John of the Cross, *The Sayings of Light and Love*, No. 100, *The Collected Works of St. John of the Cross*, translated by Kieran Kavanaugh, O.C.D., and Otilio Rodriguez, O.C.D. (Washington, DC: ICS Publications, 1991), p. 92.

[97] Acts 17:28.

and changes. Until we make the necessary changes, whether that is switching off the television, entering into silence, or avoiding a hectic life, prayer will be little more than a supplement to life, whereas it is supposed to become Life.

5. FAITHFULNESS IS THE TECHNIQUE OF REAL PRAYER

Eager willingness is not necessary in order to pray. **Prayer requires a resolution, an expression of choice on our part**. When we pray despite our reluctance, fatigue, or nervousness, we are confirming once more: "Yes, I want Your Life." **God will not change us without our input**.

Faith is therefore the basis of our prayer technique. What we do counts for far more than what we promise. Love is concrete. When we want to pray, we should determine how long and what form our daily prayers are going to take (for example, a Bible or breviary reading, reflection or meditation, saying the rosary, praying inwardly, out loud, spontaneously, and so forth) and when we are going to do this. It is also a good idea to set aside a specific place and adopt a specific posture for when we pray. Everything we specify is made an object of faith through which our faith in God Himself is thereafter expressed.

6. REAL PRAYER IS BASED ON THE WORD OF GOD: IT IS BORN OF THE WORD AND LEADS TO THE WORD

Although no two people are the same and each is guided on his own path, we have to safeguard ourselves against subjectivism in our inner life by reading the works of people who have gone before us on the road to prayer. If we base our prayers on the Bible and peruse spiritual literature, we can place our own experience within the Tradition of the Church.

7. REAL PRAYER IS SUBJECT TO PERSONAL GROWTH

Real prayer gradually becomes streamlined into a meeting that does not entail any words or impressions. We are all called to the simplest form of prayer. Tradition calls this contemplation. Every so often, it is worth considering whether our form of praying has been nourishing us and whether we need to make changes in the way we pray.

If we consider the seven principles enumerated above, it will become immediately apparent that **very few people really pray**. This is sad because prayer is meant to affect an individual's personal growth in every sphere – spiritual, physical, and emotional.

The academic literature on psychology now contains many studies confirming the healing properties of prayer. **The very act of praying has an impact on mental integration. Many academics of whatever worldview concur in this. Studies demonstrate that contemplation (called "meditation" in other circles) has a particularly beneficial impact on the psyche**. A person who practices contemplative prayer every day becomes less neurotic (increasingly freer internally and less self-absorbed), experiences less anxiety, enters into more fruitful relationships, is more understanding and gentle, assesses reality more soberly, and works more productively.[98] This comes from being able to medically verify an improvement in parameters such as blood pressure, cellular immunity, and biochemical factors. A person who meditates regularly is simply healthier. So how does that work?

This is very easily explained by disregarding theological justifications and staying entirely within the natural (that is, psychological) order. A person engaged in contemplation or

---

[98] They were quick to observe that businesspeople in many companies now try to introduce meditation practices as part of their training.

meditation, refocuses all thoughts and impressions. In this way, her thoughts become increasingly free of schemes and defense mechanisms, along with the intellectual pathways trodden by the FALSE SELF since childhood. Many people who are not necessarily Christians experience the healing effects of meditation, because it guides their consciousness towards the realm of the REAL SELF. People who pray regularly obtain the benefits mentioned above from the natural order alone.

*We have observed a dramatic improvement in emotional health and quality of life, and even a rapid recovery, in many patients who have engaged in contemplative prayer. Bulimia, anxiety, and deprivation neuroses, compulsive behaviors, pathological jealousy, addictions, and emotional deprivation disorder, not to mention plain immaturity, are only some of the medical conditions that are cured more quickly when the patient engages in prayer. **Praying, in and of itself, clearly improves the state of our patients. This could be considered a purely psychological process, but there is SOMETHING more.***

We accept people with very different outlooks on life in our practice, as long as they accept our way of working. Our office is not a place of conversion, but as we work with people, we obviously witness their changes on the spiritual plane as well.

For therapeutic reasons, we encourage non-religious people to take up meditative practices, which we teach as exercises of sorts. Our patients are often surprised to experience a certain depth within themselves. Some simply describe it as an encounter with a "gentle force," a "personal love" or "grace." Some, convinced that this SOMETHING is benevolent towards them, is concerned for their welfare, and wants them to grow, engage in prayer before the altar to the "Unknown God,"[99] and even yearn to embark on

---

[99] Cf. Acts 17:23.

a sacramental life. We might add here that this happens without any influence or encouragement on our part.

As Christians, this does not surprise us. We do not have to grope in the dark, because we are fortunate enough to have experienced a revelation in the person of Jesus. He announced that, together with the Father, he would dwell inside the individual.[100] We do not perform concentration exercises when we pray. And we enter a communion, not a void. We therefore mostly see a miraculous quality in contemplation. This stems from the fact that by praying, we are committing ourselves to working together with grace. A mysterious exchange, a sort of "heart transplant," can then be effected within us. We are not talking about improving our lives, but about something radically new that will astonish us. This happens extra-intellectually, in the obscurity of faith, when our minds are "switched off" as it were. We then witness what the Catechism of the Catholic Church says: **"Seek in reading and you will find in meditating; knock in mental prayer and it will be opened to you by contemplation."**[101]

---

[100] "Jesus answered and said to him, "Whoever loves me will keep my word, and my Father will love him, and we will come to him, and make our dwelling with him." (Jn. 14:23)

[101] Catholic Church. Catechism of the Catholic Church. 2nd ed. Vatican: Libreria Editrice Vaticana, 2012. Para. 2654

XII.

RESOLUTIONS

We have outlined five areas worth taking up, beginning by consciously working with grace. In our view, these are vitally significant for human development. They are:

- insight (self-perception);

- working with thoughts;

- actively and passively smashing adverse defense mechanisms;

- love;

- inner life (prayer).

It would be remiss of us not to propose a simple method of self-development that gives the Word a chance of being made flesh in our lives. This personal growth tool is available to anyone who wants to use it.

Let's say it once more, just to be sure:

1. THE PURPOSE OF SELF-DEVELOPMENT AND THE MOTIVATION TO TAKE IT UP

The only legitimate motive for embarking on self-development is love (of our neighbor, God, and ourselves). And **its purpose cannot be self-satisfaction** - quite the opposite. Self-development takes us to ground zero. This is where we really feel that we are powerless and vulnerable. Only this experience of humility gives us the capacity for grace.

Self-development is not concerned with our perfection, but love. We engage in it in order to love better, and not to eliminate our imperfections. Life is like gardening. We will not be judged on how many weeds we pulled out, but on how much fruit we have brought into the world. We should not become our own goal and beneficiary of our self-development.

2.   HOW TO MAKE THE RIGHT RESOLUTIONS

When we tend a fire, we are not concerned that some of the wood remains unburned. The main thing is that we fan it where the flames are already glowing. We treat self-development similarly. We should first of all operate in an area in which it is possible to do so, and not in a field of endless failures. This is by no means meant to imply that we condone sin, which we should always oppose. However, when making resolutions, **we need to choose them in an area where we can do some good.** It often happens that someone who has attended to the love of another person in earnest, unexpectedly achieves success in spheres that had, up to that point, been a string of failures. We can all unselfishly give something to another person, even if we have enormous shortcomings ourselves. Love sets us free.

We need a little time to make the right resolutions. A good time to start would be as soon as you have finished this book. Other good times are retreats, spending a day or two in silence, or a long stay in the bosom of nature, if you are receptive to its beauty. It is important that you have a couple of hours (at least) and that you do not rush. Begin by asking for the grace of good ideas, inspiration, and proposals.

We encourage you to make three resolutions concerning:

- **Loving your neighbor** (What you can do to make those around you feel more loved by you, in a mature manner, furthering their personal growth);

- **Fighting the FALSE SELF** (What can you do to become a freer person? What practices will most effectively strike at your defense mechanisms?);

- **Your inner life** (according to what has been said here concerning real prayer).

3.   WHAT QUALITIES SHOULD YOUR RESOLUTIONS HAVE?

Resolutions should be verifiable, with clearly defined endpoints. For example, resolve, "I'm going to go running on Tuesdays and Thursdays," not "I'm going to try to do more exercise;" or "The first thing I'm going to do when I get to work every day is speak to a colleague, and I'm going to tell a joke once a week," not "I'm going to try to talk more in company."

They should depend on **regularly doing something new** rather than not doing something: "I'm going to rest for half an hour every day," not "I'm not going to yell at my kids," if I suspect that my shouting is due to fatigue; or "I'm going to say something nice about my mother-in-law every day, and call her for no particular reason once a month," not "I'm not going to speak ill of my mother-in-law."

Resolutions should **demand a certain amount of effort**, but **should not be inordinately difficult.** For example, if you have never prayed regularly, don't resolve to pray for half an hour every day, but start with 15 minutes. They should be **realizable, at least once a week** (though more frequently would be better), and solely dependent on you, and not on the weather, or people close to you, and so on.

4. WHAT ABOUT MAKING SOME CHANGES?

In addition to long-term resolutions, we can also experience a strong and sudden inspiration to pursue a particular course in life, such as "I'm going to start therapy," "I'm going to change my major or quit my job," "I'm going to move," etc. Such urges have to be subjected to calm and leisurely analysis and reflection in line with what is written in the chapter on changes.

We make prayer or spiritual resolutions at least every six months, or for a year at a time. This can be done during a certain time of year, such as Advent, or while on vacation. It is important that these resolutions be very specific and something that we can adhere to. We then take stock of our lives when the specified time has elapsed. It may be that it is worth continuing with a particular resolution. Then again, it may be time to take on something completely new.

And we can repeat this evaluating of our endeavors in this manner for the rest of our days!

"They that sow in tears shall reap in joy"

Working with grace is extraordinarily beautiful. Self-development is an illuminated hope for resurrection. It will cost a little effort, but it pays back so much more inner freedom and fruits of the Spirit that it becomes a source of ever-greater joy. The closer we get to the Truth, the more eagerly we jettison the ballast of our misguided attitudes and convictions, and the more enthusiastically we throw ourselves into the fight against whatever remains of the old person inside us. The hardest part is getting started: "Those who sow in tears will reap with cries of joy. Those who go forth weeping, carrying sacks of seed, will return with cries of joy, carrying their bundled sheaves."[102]

I look back and smile, although it hurt.

Now I can see: It all made sense – something's recovered,

Finally standing at Your gates, so transparent,

That my heart is free in itself and my senses liberated.

If I find myself that safe under the breath of life,

Able to embrace all I've already felt with a glance.

The ancient gates then open with a crash,

---

[102] Psalm 126: 5-6.

And I hope, and believe, that we'll all meet up there sometime.

When I stand there joyously with empty hands,

The veil is torn, free now in Your temple.

I know all things with a known meaning,

I choose love, as I myself am chosen.[103]

In memory of St. Therese of the Child Jesus,

in the Fire of Light and Love.

Olsza, 1 October 2012.

---

[103] These are the lyrics of the song " Patrzę do tyłu, uśmiecham się" [I look back and smile] from Marcin's album Milczę i kocham [I remain silent and love].

Bibliography

We find ourselves in some difficulty here. This book has its origin in many and varied sources. We received some of our ideas directly from the hands of grace. Others came from people. We have internalized and transformed the substance of what we have heard and read over the years. It has become increasingly difficult to trace our human sources. It might even be at times that a concept we treat as our own original idea might actually have been conveyed to us by someone else. We have frequently been delighted to find that other writers think similarly to us. This is why this book has so few footnotes. We realize that this is a weakness (and by no means the only one), but our intention was not to write a textbook. We apologize to all the writers and educators we have listed here "wholesale," without detailed references. Anyone we have omitted to mention can rest assured that we have not done so through malice. We take this opportunity to give anyone the right to cite and use the ideas contained herein. Everything is freely available: "And what do you possess that you have not received?"[104]

We would especially like to thank Sr. Miriam of the Cross, whose love, prayers, and words have accompanied us for many years. It would be impossible to do justice to the wealth of correspondence and personal communication from her and with her here. We would also like to express our gratitude to all those writers who have gone before us in seeking love and goodness in the service of human growth. We have additionally included those with whom we do not identify philosophically, academically, or in terms of outlook, but

---

[104] Cf. 1 Cor 4:7.

who have nevertheless got us thinking and helped us mature. We are grateful to them too.

We have read all the works listed below and each of them has influenced our thinking to a greater or lesser extent.

Abba, powiedz mi słowo. Wybór apoftegmatów. Kraków, 1997.

Aleksandrowicz J. W. Psychoterapia medyczna. Warszaw, 1996.

Amorth G. Egzorcyści i psychiatrzy. Częstochowa, 1999.

Bielecki J.E. OCD. Temperament a świętość. Kraków, 1999.

Brat Wawrzyniec od zmartwychwstania OCD. O praktykowaniu Bożej obecności. Kraków, 2007.

Carnes P. Od nałogu do miłości. Poznań, 2001.

Cohen R., M.A. Wyjść na prostą. Rozumienie i uzdrowienie homoseksualizmu. Kraków, 2002.

Croissant J. Ciało świątynią bożego piękna. Kraków, 1999.

Daigneault A. Droga niedoskonałości. Kraków, 2010.

Działa E. OP. Skrupulantom na ratunek. Poznań, 2002.

Ellis A. Terapia krótkoterminowa, lepiej, głębiej, trwalej. Gdańsk, 1998.

Eugeniusz Maria od Dzieciątka Jezus OCD. Chcę widziec Boga. Kraków, 1998.

Eugeniusz Maria od Dzieciątka Jezus OCD. Jestem córką Kościoła. Kraków, 1984.

Fromm E. Mieć czy być? Poznań, 2007.

Garrigou-Lagrange R. OP. Trzy okresy życia wewnętrznego. Niepokalanów, 2001.

Grün A. O duchowości inaczej. Kraków, 2009.

Grün A. i Robben M.M. Znajdź własną drogę. Kielce, 2003.

Grzywocz K. Zeszyty Formacji Duchowej nr 41. Uczucia niekochane. Kraków, 2008

Hellinger B. Porządki miłości, czyli być sobą i żyć swoim życiem. Warszawa, 2006.

Horney K. Nerwica a rozwój człowieka. Poznań, 2006.

Houston G. Gestalt. Terapia krótkoterminowa. Gdańsk, 2006.

Jalics F. SJ. Rekolekcje kontemplatywne. Kraków, 2008.

Kappert D. Archetypy, symbolika ciała, obrazy wewnętrzne. Warszawa, 2004.

Katechizm Kościoła Katolickiego. Poznań, 1994.

Keating T. OCSO. Otwarty umysł otwarte serce. Poznań, 2004.

Kępiński A. Melancholia. Kraków, 1993.

Kępiński A. Rytm życia. Kraków, 1973.

Kępiński A. Z psychopatologii życia seksualnego. Kraków, 1992.

Kilpatrick W.K. Psychologiczne uwiedzenie. Czy psychologia zastąpi religię? Poznań, 2007.

Krzyżowski J. Depresja. Warszawa, 2002.

Krzyżowski J. Natręctwa, obsesje i kompulsje. Warszawa, 2003.

Krzyżowski J. Stany lękowe. Warszawa, 2005.

Kutter P. Współczesna psychoanaliza. Gdańsk, 1998.

Lowen A. i Lowen L. Droga do zdrowia i witalności. Koszalin, 2011.

Manne J. Psychologia buddyjska w codziennym życiu. Warszawa, 2010.

Medinger A. Podróż ku pełni męskości. Poznań, 2005.

Merton T. OCSO. Chleb na pustyni. Kraków, 1998.

Merton T. OCSO. Modlitwa kontemplacyjna. Poznań, 1986.

Merton T. OCSO. Posiew kontemplacji. Nikt nie jest samotną wyspą. Kraków, 1989.

Merton T. OCSO. Siedmiopiętrowa góra. Poznań, 1998.

Merton T. OCSO. Życie w milczeniu. Kraków, 1991.

Modlitwa nieustanna. Konferencje wygłoszone przez Siostrę Miriam od Krzyża dla wspólnoty Sióstr Karmelitanek Bosych w Szczecinie (1997). Poznań, 2008.

Namysłowska I. Terapia rodzin. Warszawa, 1997.

Nicolosi, J.J. Wstyd i utrata przywiązania. Bydgoszcz, 2011.

Obłok niewiedzy. Poznań, 1986.

Payne L. Zniszczony obraz. Gorzów Wlkp., 2005.

Peck M. Scott. Droga rzadziej wędrowana. Poznań, 2006.

Pennington M.B. OCSO. Modlitwa prowadząca do środka. Kraków, 2003.

Półtawska W. Beskidzkie rekolekcje. Częstochowa, 2009.

Psychoterapia tańcem i ruchem. Praca zbiorowa pod redakcją Z. Pędzich. Warszawa, 2009.

Rohr R. OFM. Wszystko ma swoje miejsce. Kraków, 2008.

Rohr R. i Ebert A. Enneagram. Dziewięć typów osobowości. Kraków, 2004.

Siegel R.D. Uważność. Trening pokonywania codziennych trudności. Warszawa, 2011.

Stinissen W. OCD. Ani Joga ani Zen. Poznań, 2000.

Stinissen W. OCD. Noc jest mi światłem. Kraków, 2004.

Stinissen W. OCD. Panie naucz nas modlić się. Ku modlitwie milczenia. Poznań, 2003.

Stinissen W. OCD. Prosta droga do świętości - śladem św. Teresy z Lisieux. Poznań, 2001.

Stinissen W. OCD. Wędrówka wewnętrzna. Poznań, 2001.

Stinissen W. OCD. Wieczność pośrodku czasu. Poznań, 1997.

Św. Jan od Krzyża. Dzieła. Kraków, 1986.

Św. Teresa od Dzieciątka Jezus. Dzieje duszy. Kraków, 1984.

Terruwe A.A. i Baars C.W. Integracja emocjonalna, jak uwierzyć, że jesteś kochany i potrafisz kochać. Poznań, 2004.

Terruwe A.A. i Baars C.W. Integracja psychiczna. Warszawa, 2002.

Vanier J. Wspólnota miejscem radości i przebaczenia. Warszawa, 1991.

Wojtyła K. Miłość i odpowiedzialność. Lublin, 1986.

BY THE SAME AUTHORS:

1. *Wolny w ramionach najwyższego,*
   Pieśni CD, Pro homine, Bolechowo, 2007.

2. *Milczę i kocham,*
   Pieśni CD, Pro homine, Bolechowo, 2010.

3. *Rodzice w akcji,* - Book and audiobook.
   Edycja Św. Pawła, Kraków, 2011.

4. *Wprowadzenie do modlitwy kontemplacyjnej,*
   Pro homine, Szczecin, 2012.

5. *Nie przerywając ciszy,*
   Pieśni CD, Pro homine, Bolechowo, 2014.

6. *Zrozumienie, współczucie,*
   Pieśni CD, Pro homine, Bolechowo, 2014.

7. *Rozwój. Jak współpracować z łaską? - Audiobook,*
   Pro homine, Bolechowo, 2015.

8. *Świątynia. Wprowadzenie do kontemplacji*
   Pro homine, Bolechowo, 2018.

9. *Rodzice nastolatków w akcji,* - Audiobook,
   Pro homine, Bolechowo, 2020.

TThe authors' websites in Polish:

www.gajdy.pl

Books and CDs by Monika and Marcin Gajda are available for purchase, and there is current information on the initiatives, retreats, workshops, and conferences they run.

www.przyjacielemm.pl

This is the webpage of the Przyjaciele Miłości Miłosiernej (Friends of Merciful Love), a spiritual family set up by the authors to gather people who want to live in contemplative spirituality ("the spirituality of empty hands"). The site has information on contemplative prayer groups that meet in various cit es in Poland. You can also download religious instruction, and conferences on spirituality and personal growth, or listen online.

www.terapia-szczecin.pl

This is the webpage of the "Pro Homine" Psychotherapy and Advice Center. This is a place where therapists who practice Christian Integrated Therapy come together.